The Best of Us

Life Lessons from Youth Work

By Paul Oginsky and Jo Hawley

For all the incredible youth workers out there - thank you

Support for the book

"Youth workers are masters of personal and social development. The world is rapidly changing, and their refreshing approach can help everyone achieve and find their 'A' game. This book is much needed and most welcome."

Dame Kelly Holmes DBE OLY,
President of the Dame Kelly Holmes Trust

"Youth workers transform lives. Whoever you are, the insights here will help you transform yours."

Simon Weston CBE, Falklands Veteran and Weston Spirit

"Life doesn't come with an instruction manual, but if it did, it would look a lot like this book. It's packed with practical wisdom, powerful insights, and step-by-step guidance to help you reach new heights. A true roadmap for success and fulfilment!"

Robin Sieger, Author of the Best-Selling Book Natural Born Winners and International Keynote Business Speaker

Disclaimer

We have been advised to write a disclaimer, so here goes. All the people and events described in this book are true and accurate according to our memories. That is how we remember things occurring. More or less. If, however, you appear in the book and remember things differently, you may well be right. Please accept our apology. We meant no harm. If you are still annoyed, please re-read the chapter on conflict resolution, it should help. Names have been changed to protect identities.

Contents

Becoming the Best of Us:
Why you need this book now

The future of the human race feels increasingly uncertain. After decades of positive economic and geopolitical progress, for the first time in a long time, the next generation cannot expect a better quality of life than their parents. The world has become a more complicated place. The internet and social media have not brought our communities closer together but seem to have driven people farther apart. Never have our communities been more fractured.

Despite all the progress we have made in our civilisations, we are still fighting wars. Conflict, climate and economic changes have caused unexpected immigration flows for which destination countries have been ill-prepared. Through both boom times and busts, we create billionaires whilst others starve. Technology races ahead. Artificial Intelligence and quantum computing promise further advances but will create unprecedented change. Meanwhile climate change threatens our very existence as a species.

This new reality presents new challenges to us both personally and professionally. Our family units – long seen as the bedrock of a civilised society – are under immense pressure as never before with parents often feeling helpless to know how to support their children to meet the ever-changing demands the modern world throws at our young people. Professionally, we need to lead people through a period of change and uncertainty, but are struggling to get to grips with hybrid working and can't figure out how to motivate Generation Z.

Have we depressed you? Fear not! We are here to help, because to survive - in fact thrive - in this emerging new world, we must develop into the very best we can be as human beings. We need to improve our relationships, boost our resilience, improve our critical thinking and much more besides. Much of this - most of what we will help you develop throughout the course of this book - has often been considered "soft skills" and not the focus of mainstream education systems. But they are in fact the essential attributes for facing the future.

How do we know this? Well, we've seen these skills and attributes in action. In the field of youth work.

Youth work has long been a misunderstood and underrated profession. But those working in the youth field have developed a philosophy and a methodology that can bring out the 'best of us' individually and as a species. We will say much more about all this, but essentially, those who invest in their own personal and social development, and those who support the personal and social development of others, will gain the benefits.

But before we go any further, let us introduce ourselves properly.

Paul: My name is Paul Oginsky and for the last 30 years I have been working with young people who have needed a bit of extra help to succeed in life. It's become increasingly clear to me that everyone - no matter what profession, age or background - could learn a lot from the world of youth workers. Who else can talk around a bunch of frustrated teenagers? Who else walks towards a tough situation like that? There's a lot we can learn from the people who regularly face seemingly impossible challenges. I'm also a parent and a grandparent, using this skillset to try to navigate family life too.

Jo: My name is Jo Hawley. I'm a senior civil servant who has had a wide variety of roles over the last 25 years, working on everything from gritty child protection cases to far-flung diplomatic postings. For several years, I worked closely with the youth sector, which is where I came across some of the most inspiring people you could ever hope to meet - including Paul. Where others wrote-off vulnerable young people as just too difficult, youth workers - these modest heroes - would turn lives and communities around. It was immediately clear to me that I had a lot to learn from these incredibly talented individuals and what I have learnt has helped me immeasurably in the world of management, leadership and international diplomacy.

Paul & Jo: Between us, we are going to take you on a journey through the chapters of this book. We have distilled in these pages 10 key attributes the are demonstrated by excellent youth workers. We believe that you - whatever your walk of life - can learn to use them effectively and apply them in areas of your personal and professional life and that this will help you face the new challenges our changing world is throwing at you. Maybe you've read Stephen R. Covey's *The 7 Habits of Highly Effective People*? Well, this is like the 10 habits of highly effective youth workers, except that everyone can benefit from these skills, and they are exactly what is needed now and for the years to come.

Paul: My professional life has regularly thrown up new and unforeseen challenges, but I have a crucial lever which helps me tackle any challenge: amazing youth work skills. Now I'm not saying that all youth workers are amazing. But the really great ones have a magic touch which can turn around the lives of some of the hardest to reach young people. And as we've discussed, we can all take a few lessons from that.

Paul & Jo: Great youth workers transform lives, transform communities. But who are these people? How do they do it? And why aren't more of us using these skills?

That's why we have written this book. In so many contexts, professional and personal, we increasingly see opportunities for deploying key youth work skills: to face new challenges, to improve the world around us and improve ourselves, our own opportunities and those of others. But most of us don't do this, as not all of the key attributes of amazing youth work are well-developed tools in our toolbox. We have not been trained, have not developed these skills sufficiently, do not always recognise when we should reach for them, do not know how to best use them.

In writing this book, we have reached out to some of the best youth workers we know to really help distil down the key attributes that great youth workers have and that the rest of us need to develop to improve our interactions with others. Over the chapters of this book, we will introduce you to the 10 key attributes and take you on a journey, through stories and practical exercises, to help you develop and benefit from them in your day-to-day life.

We are not saying that teachers and police officers need to transform into youth workers. A teacher needs to impart knowledge, and a police officer will often need to lay down the law. But what we are saying is that if teachers and police officers had a few more youth worker skills and knew how and when to deploy them, they'd ultimately be more effective in delivering their core objectives.

Likewise, we are not saying that youth workers would make great FTSE 100 CEOs. But we truly believe that each of those CEOs could learn valuable lessons from youth workers. These skills can also make us better parents and partners. Great youth workers have a lot of teach us all in how to have better interactions with others.

If we all - personally and professionally - learn to use these skills at the right time, it will help us face what the future challenges with confidence, will improve our relationships, our effectiveness, and our results. They will help us become the best versions of ourselves.

What do we mean by *youth work* and *youth workers?*

In literal terms *youth worker* means anyone who works with young people. This could include teachers, health workers, police officers, sports coaches etc. In the UK however, the term *youth worker* identifies adults who are employed or who work voluntarily to engage and develop young people. There are training courses, qualifications and agreed standards for people who specialise in this purpose. Not everyone who provides engaging activities for young people can be said to be doing *youth work*. Sometimes sport, art, drama, cadets and dance clubs for example are more leisure and fun-focused, rather than developmental, though of course they can have positive impacts on character development.

For the purpose of this book, we define *youth work* as a process of building relationships with young people so as to enhance their personal and social development.

Lessons from Youth Work

So now let's take the first step on this development journey together and look in more detail at three examples of great youth work in action and the incredible results which can be achieved.

Throughout this book, we'll pose questions to get you to reflect on the lessons we are sharing. We suggest making a few notes to help you explore the questions thoroughly. As you read these stories consider:

- Do you agree with the approach taken?
- What would you have done if you were in that situation?
- What skills did the youth workers show?
- How might the skills be used to improve your own life?

Lessons from Youth Work: Story 1

"Being considerate of others will take your children further in life than any college degree." Marian Wright Edelman

Two teenage girls approached a youth worker in Newcastle one day. They said they were concerned about a friend's safety and didn't know what to do. The youth worker informed the girls that she was duty bound to act on information if someone's safety was being jeopardised. The girls spoke to each other and decided to tell the youth worker their concerns.

A boy (who we will name Todd) had been in a school sports lesson playing football and had kicked the ball into the groin of another lad (who we will call Carl). Todd went on to score. This was mildly embarrassing for Carl but not too serious at this stage. The problem was that Carl's friends provoked him into confronting Todd. Todd was a thoughtful and quiet young man who didn't want any trouble, so he had walked away, but Carl's friends warmed to their theme and wouldn't let it lie.

The girls - one of whom had a boyfriend in Carl's circle - had become aware of a plan for Carl and his friends to stab Todd at the youth centre that evening.

The youth worker thanked the girls for telling her and told them they had done the right thing. The youth worker was part of a multi-agency network, which was set up to protect vulnerable young people and included the police, social services and schools. Through the school, Todd's parents were contacted, and he was told not to attend the youth centre that evening. Carl's parents (who were known to social services) were also contacted but said that they did not know where Carl was.

The police visited the youth centre that evening but everything was quiet and so they left. An hour later Carl arrived with a group of five other teenage boys. They went through the youth centre and sat in the garden at the back. There was only one way in and out of the centre, so the youth worker called the police. When the police arrived, they waited by the front door.

The youth worker then went out and spoke to the lads herself in the garden. She explained that she had heard rumour that they had been threatening Todd. She said that there were police at the door and if anything happened to Todd, they would be prime suspects. Carl and his mates professed their innocence, saying they had no problem with Todd.

They left the building and walked past the police officers who searched them, finding nothing.

The school brought both sets of parents and the two lads together the next day. Hands were shaken and peace resumed.

A couple of days later the youth worker found two knives buried in the ground where the lads had been sitting. The brave and sensitive work of the youth worker, coordinating this wider team, had altered the course of many lives that day.

Lessons from Youth Work: Story 2

"Tough times don't last, tough teams do." Robert Schuller

Paul: My team and I once took a group of twenty teenagers from Liverpool to the Derbyshire countryside on a seven-day residential course. This wasn't our first rodeo. I had a strong staff team who had worked together many times and knew what to expect from a residential course. The late nights, the risks of putting teenagers together overnight without parents around, the mischievous aim to get one over on the staff. But, oh my goodness, this group were extra challenging!

We set them plenty of team tasks, but they failed all of them, over and again. They just would not work as a team. They wouldn't listen to each other; they wouldn't co-operate, and they would argue over the tiniest little thing.

I called a staff meeting and we decided to hold a special team task. Our thinking was that they had too much energy to co-operate so we would keep them busy until 10pm, then send them to bed, let them fall asleep, but wake them up at midnight to find and rescue one of the staff (who would be hiding in a nearby field).

Things were going to plan. The group went to bed shattered and once they fell quiet and the lights went off, I picked a member of my team to go hide. I decided on a guy named Simon Weston - a tough Falklands war veteran. I wanted someone hardy as it was midwinter and with this particular group of teenagers as his rescue team, he was likely to be out there for some time!

Simon disappeared into the dark and the plan was for us to wait 20 minutes before giving the group their rude awakening. During this time however, the heavens opened, and rain came down in biblical proportions. I knew that Simon could take a lot, but I didn't want to leave him out there too long in this weather, so we went to get the group up right away. This is when the plan fell apart.

The bedrooms were empty. The group where nowhere to be found. All twenty of them had gone. I had responsibility for twenty teenagers on a horrendous winter's night and I had no idea where they were. It turned out that they had climbed out of the back window and crept off to the late-night shop in the local village.

As we stood in their empty dormitory, we heard them scrambling around behind the building trying to get back in. We put the lights on and caught them all standing at the back of the room like a scene from *The Colditz Story*. Only the cans of beer and bottles of cider ruined the picture.

"Go to the main room," I said in a low, threatening voice. They knew they were nicked and with uncharacteristic compliance, they walked crest-fallen through the rain and sat in a circle in the main room. I walked in with the staff at my side. The group of young people had all explicitly agreed, as a qualification for coming onto the course, not to drink. We were genuinely disappointed with them, and the group could tell.

"Put the booze on the table," I said. The group shuffled and filled the table, bottles clinking. "If we can't trust you, we can't continue." The group could tell I was deadly serious. They were stunned, shocked and emotional.

I found their reaction encouraging. It showed they wanted to be there. That gave me something to work with. "It's late. Go to bed and we will talk about it in the morning." The group went to bed, genuinely gutted and ashamed. The staff gathered around, delighted by their reaction! We were finally getting somewhere with this group.

(Oh, and it was at this point the door burst open and there stood a drenched, sneezing Simon Weston. Looking around the room he saw the happy staff and smiling at each other, a table full of drink. "What the hell is going on?" He exclaimed, assuming we had played a sick joke on him!)

The next morning the group were on their best behaviour, not wanting to be sent home. They had obviously had a group discussion, and their attitude had changed. The staff appreciated the offers of cups of coffee, toast and a politeness comparable to staying at a high-end hotel!

Now that the group were more compliant, we wanted to push them so that they gained a sense of achievement. After breakfast we sat with the group, as they awaited our decision. I explained that we needed to see them work as a team and therefore we had set them a difficult team task. Pass and stay. Fail and go home. You can't bluff young people, so we had agreed this as a staff team. We were playing this for real.

We had to set a task that that would challenge the group - but that was achievable - as we didn't really want to send them home. We had an assault course on site, so we set them one of our favourite tasks. The group had to make it around the assault course in a set time. Anyone not over the line in time was going home.

To make the task more challenging we gave each member of the group a random handicap. Five were told they couldn't speak, five were blindfolded, five weren't allowed to walk and five couldn't use their arms (we tied them behind their backs). This was a tough challenge on this assault course, but this was a tough group.

They showed absolute determination when standing on the start line. The five who couldn't walk sat on the floor.

"Go!" I shouted and the ones who "just" couldn't speak shot off, leaving the more physically challenged in their dust.

"Get back here!" Screamed Christine, one of the girls who had her hands bound. She was loud, funny and more than a little bit scary, so the mute group sheepishly returned. "Now listen," said Christine stepping in to the leadership role. "If we are going to get through this we are going to have to work together." And with that group started to work as a team. The way they negotiated the 2-metre wall was impressive. Christine sat on top of the wall barking instructions while the "blind" and "mute" youngsters lifted the "legless" and "armless" safely over the wall.

The next obstacle was the pit which meant they all had to submerge in freezing muddy water. It started to look like a first world war scene. The shouts and encouragement died away as the cold and the pain began to bite.

Time was running out as the team faced the log. This was a long telegraph pole over a pond that was muddy and slippery to walk across. Most of the team had made it across but one "armless" girl was really struggling. She had her legs either side of the pole but was nearly slipping into the water "Come on, girl," shouted Christine. "Use your f*nny as a sucker!" The group cracked up and the girl did well not to fall off the log laughing.

With just seconds left, it was a sprint to the finish line. The staff gave a count down from 10 seconds. One lad with "no legs" was pulling himself, two of the silent teenagers carried another towards the line. The count got to 4...3...2...

With one monumental effort the group fell over the line as we shouted "Stop!" There was silence, as the group looked at me for the result. Did they all make it?

"Congratulations!" I said. "You did it!"

The cheers were amazing. However this group was doing in school, whatever people thought of their chances in life, they were winners in our eyes and more importantly they were winners in their own eyes. The bond that was formed on that residential course formed lifelong friendships. I still see them occasionally and they set up a Facebook page where they post updates to each other. They are doing well.

To get the most out of tough young people you need to give them tough challenges. Perhaps that's what we all need.

Lessons from Youth Work: Story 3

"Stand for what is right. Even if it means standing alone." Suzy Kassem

A great youth worker who deserves more recognition is an impressive lady called Sara Rowbotham.
As a front-line sexual health worker, Sara was working out of a community centre in Rochdale in 2004, when a 14-year-old girl who was attending the

centre reported to Sara that she had a new boyfriend. Alarm bells started to ring for Sara when the girl said her boyfriend was a taxi driver. Further alarm bells rang when other girls who attended the centre reported that they were attending parties with this taxi driver and other men.

Sara reported her concerns to her seniors and the police, but little action was taken. It was a sensitive situation. The men were of Pakistani origin and the right-wing English Defence League (EDL) was on the rise in the area. The police did not want to enflame the situation. But at the end of the day, vulnerable young girls were being abused. Sara could not accept that. She called a meeting with fellow youth work professionals, and they decided to set up an incident room. The wall looked like something out of a movie with names, photos and connecting stories, victims and perpetrators. Through this work, Sara uncovered evidence that suggested that this was a co-ordinated network of men running a paedophile ring.

Sara went to the press, the Crown Prosecution Service and even her MP. She raised so much attention that it couldn't be ignored.

The girls finally got the support they needed, the men were prosecuted and in 2012 were sent to prison. Several paedophile networks across the northwest of England were identified and shut down. Countless young girls were saved.

In 2014, Sara was made redundant. But she didn't let that stop her. She went on to be elected as deputy leader of Rochdale Council.

Clarity of purpose will carry you through.

Consider the questions again having read these case studies and make a few notes:

- Do you agree with the approach taken?

- What would you have done if you were in that situation?

- What skills did the youth workers show?

- How might the skills be used to improve your own life?

Great youth workers really are amongst The Best of Us. But how have youth workers developed such skills?

The context of their work is complex and challenging:

1. *The people who need the service the most don't want it.*

Youth workers often work with young people who are displaying challenging, risk taking, anti-social and sometimes criminal behaviours. They don't usually welcome adults into their social circle. Who in their right mind would sign up for a job like that?! Youth workers then have to be answerable for their tricky-to-measure outcomes. They must prove something which is very unscientific: stopping bad things happening and making good things happen. This requires them to be convincing and persuasive, but with high levels of integrity.

2. *Youth workers must build strong and friendly relationships, but not become friends.*

Youth workers walk a tricky line of being friendly with young people without getting caught up in the conflicts that could stem from being friends with their clients. They work within the framework of the law and as well as addressing the needs of young people, youth workers have a range of responsibilities to other people, including other youth workers, family members, funders, schools, the police and other services and the wider community.

3. *Youth workers must know when to be passive, active, proactive, reactive.*

While a good youth worker may look relaxed, they are noticing everything. How the mood is changing, if the energy is positive or negative and what is likely to happen in the coming moments, hours, weeks or months. Are there dangers or opportunities? Intervene too quickly or too often and they will lose the trust of the group. Intervene too late and someone could get seriously hurt or even worse. They are constantly seeking to find the right balance.

4. *Youth workers are judged by the decisions other people make.*
Young people can sometimes make awful decisions driven by adrenaline, peer-pressure or curiosity, often without concern for the consequences. A youth worker's aim is for the young people to make more effective choices. It is therefore on the actions of others that the success of a youth worker is judged.

It's quite the job description! In today's world people who are credible, persuasive, professional and vigilant are worth their weight in gold. Thankfully many such people have found their way into the youth sector. It is from incredible stories and wonderful people like these that we have distilled the following 10 lessons to take you - the reader - on the journey of developing your effectiveness to help you meet the challenges that the world is providing. Lessons that will help you become one of *The Best of Us.*

Let's look now at the first of these 10 attributes: youth workers see themselves as *always learning.* They recognise that they are not the final product, but on a developmental journey. By reading this book, undertaking this journey of self-development, you too are on this path already! Now let us help you along it a little further.

Attribute 1: Always Learning

Socrates emphasised the importance of continuous learning and humility in his famous statement: *"The only true wisdom is knowing you know nothing."*

Since he was possibly the greatest philosopher in antiquity, we of course don't take this at face value. Clearly the great man knew a great deal! But a key technique he used to debate problems involved the use of skilful questions and posing interesting dilemmas to help see things from a different perspective. This is exactly what great youth workers do! And indeed, what we are seeking to do in this book.

This self-renewal is crucial when faced with an uncertain future. We can't rely on the skills and experiences we have used before to succeed in the new reality. We need to develop new skills, new approaches, new mindsets.

Any development journey needs to start with a look at oneself. This is something that great youth workers do continuously. They never see themselves as the final product. They recognise that each of us is on a learning journey and - crucially for their work - they do not believe that they have all the answers just because they have been on their journey longer than their young clients have.

Paul: This development journey we are all on can be termed *personal and social development*, which I define as a process by which we learn from our experiences and become more effective in our decisions and relationships. We are effective when we align our beliefs, values and actions.

By undertaking *personal and social development*, we improve our character. This is why it is sometimes referred to as *character education*.

Character development can happen any time, any place. A young person can have a row with a friend, make a realisation and change the way they live their life forever. Great youth workers support young people on this journey, whilst recognising that they are still very much on the path themselves and don't have all the answers.

One of the best youth workers I've ever had the privilege to work alongside is Greg Falola. His interpersonal skills are phenomenal. If you ever need someone to deal with a tricky client, Greg is your man. Greg isn't perhaps the most academically gifted. Spelling is a particular challenge for him and youth workers often have to write on whiteboards in front of a group. But Greg actually uses his weakness as a strength for engaging his audience. He explains to the group that his spelling is bad and the reaction from the young people is often surprising. Rather than seeing weakness and going for the jugular, young people often connect with this vulnerability. They engage more. They start helping Greg, calling out the spellings for him, offering to write things on the board for him. Greg isn't afraid to admit there are things he doesn't know or can't do and that is a real strength.

The success of this approach I have also witnessed outside the youth work world. I was once invited to a gathering of about a dozen youth organisations to brainstorm ideas about how to get young people involved in protecting the environment. On the attendance list was an Army General who was doing some work with The Prince's Trust. Interesting, I thought. I wonder what a General might suggest. I was intrigued to meet him.

On the day of the meeting, we all introduced ourselves, but it seemed the General was running late. As we started into the meat of the discussion, we heard the noise of – could it be? – helicopter blades getting louder and louder. Suddenly a military chopper was landing right by our meeting room. We all stopped to look through the window in time to see the General leap down and bound over towards us, resplendent in all his military finery, a blur of gold braid and insignia. It was quite the entrance. He opened the door with a flourish, strode in, coming to each of us in turn, shaking our hands and introducing himself importantly, repeating his name to each person in a loud confident voice as he went around the room. I've never witnessed anyone enter a room with more confidence and sense of self-worth.

We sat down and the meeting restarted with us throwing around difficult challenges. Every now and again the General would go: "Tell me! Why is this happening? Why did you do this? Why did this person act like that?" His authoritative tone impacted the group who begin to act as if they were there to brief him. I was fascinated by this guy. Maybe I was feeling a bit chippy, as he was a General who swanned around in a helicopter, and we were youth organisations. (I don't always react well to heavy handed authority figures!) I thought: the next time he demands answers of us, I'm going to put the question back to him. "Why didn't this happen?" He put to one of my neighbours at the table. "Well, General," I intervened. "Why do you think it didn't happen?"

He looked at me and with a calm, confident, loud, authoritative voice said: "I don't know."

And I just thought "wow." I've never heard anyone admit they didn't know something with such authority and confidence! I realised after that that some of the most successful people are precisely that because they don't see lack of knowledge as a weakness but have a curiosity to address those gaps. Never ceasing their journey for improvement.

One day in early 2012 I was working in London when I got a call from my friend Nick Van Breemen. Nick was a charity fundraiser, and we had worked together for many years. We share a sense of humour, and we usually start our telephone conversations with a joke or a silly voice. Not this time however, Nick was in a tight spot, and he needed my help.

A few months earlier Nick had organised a fundraising dinner for the Air Ambulance charity, and one of the auction prizes was a tour of the House of Commons. The auction winner was the film director Danny Boyle. Danny was in London working on the opening ceremony of the 2012 Olympics with his friend and co-creator, novelist Frank Cottrell-Boyce. The two men found they had some free time around midday that very day, and they had contacted Nick to see if they could do the tour. As it happened there were no tours scheduled for that day, but Nick knew I had a parliamentary pass and asked me if I could show them around. Given that I don't have a degree in history, and I hadn't trained as a tour guide, my 'showing them around' would have been short-changing them to say the least. I was embarrassed at the thought of my saying: "Here is a big statue and here is a bigger one." So, I went to the tour guide's office and used all my youth work skills to get them to agree a special tour just for us.

I met up with Nick, Danny and Frank at the super posh Cinnamon Club near the House of Commons, where Danny treated us all to lunch. We all got along like old friends, laughing and swapping stories. They were as curious of my work as I was about theirs. The one thing that we could not discuss was the Olympics as the opening ceremony was very hush hush. (It would be weeks before everyone would see Her Majesty jumping out of a helicopter and see Mr Bean playing in the orchestra.)

After lunch we walked to parliament and received the most fascinating tour with amazing facts which were delivered by a truly skilled and knowledgeable tour guide. At one point the guide took us down into the bowels of parliament and showed us a very small broom cupboard. It turns out that this little cupboard played a significant role in the suffragette movement.

On the night of the 1911 census, a suffragette named Emily Davison hid inside the broom cupboard. Her goal was to have her address on the census registered as "The House of Commons" to show that women should have the same political rights as men. Emily Davison famously went on to throw herself under the King's horse at the Derby and died for her cause of furthering democracy. (If I had been doing the tour, I would have said "and this is where we keep the mops.")

The tour guide explained that if we squeezed in two at a time, shut the door and turned around we would see a plaque on the back of the door (actually made and put there entirely without official permission by MP Tony Benn, who was determined to commemorate the act.) I went into the cupboard with Danny. It was really cramped, and we virtually had to hug each other to shut the door, plus it was totally dark, so I had to fiddle in my pocket to get my phone for some light. I remember thinking, I know life can be unpredictable but when I woke up this morning, I never thought I would be in a cupboard hugging Danny Boyle!

Danny gently ran his hand over the plaque as if it was an ancient Egyptian artifact. I heard him whisper to himself under his breath "We have got to include this." I knew what he meant. He was somehow going to include the story of the suffragettes in the opening ceremony. (Well, either that or he wanted to see how many athletes he could squeeze into a broom cupboard.) All the arrangements were probably already in place, but Danny was on the hunt for continual improvement. That's what makes him an amazing director and a fascinating man.

A few weeks later, on the big day itself, I settled down to watch the opening ceremony along with an estimated worldwide TV audience of over 900 million people. Sure enough, halfway through the event came a troop of woman dressed as suffragettes and the announcer told their story. I felt a rush of pride. I thought to myself: "I am really glad I pulled out the stops for Nick that day." Then I asked myself: "What can I do better tomorrow?"

In management

Jo: The advice around this key attribute of always seeking to learn, speaks to a tension in management culture: how to inspire confidence in others without closing yourself off to feedback and the input of others, especially more junior colleagues. Leaders often feel that they are under pressure to have all the answers. In a professional context, it can be dog-eat-dog with only the alphas rising to the top. Admitting you aren't the final product can be seen as showing too much vulnerability, risking loss of respect from others.

A few years ago, an experience in China helped me learn more about how to balance the need for drawing on others with instilling confidence within my team.

Having spent 20 years in the Civil Service and nearly a year into what was my 4th overseas posting, I had a certain amount of confidence that I generally knew what I was doing as new year 2020 approached. Then suddenly a strange, deadly new virus arrived in China, our offices went into crisis mode, and we had to face something for which all of us were unprepared. Or were we? My Chinese colleagues had been here before - during SARS in 2002. A frightening disease with high mortality rates had swept across the country. Indeed, the mother of one of my colleagues had been a doctor who had tragically died of SARS.

So, what I really needed were the insights of my team. But in China, advising the boss is culturally complicated. Leaders are not expected to show vulnerability or any weakness. Indeed, pointing out any areas for improvement to a senior is seen as a loss of face for all involved: loss of face to even the individual proposing the idea, as it shamefully shows that they are working for someone who isn't up to the expected standard.

This is something that a lot of leaders and managers struggle with the world over. How to inspire confidence in your team, whilst getting your colleagues to give you valuable insights and ideas. By admitting that you don't have all the answers, will you be seen as weak? I'd suggest from my experience in China, there are ways in which to go about this which deliver the right balance of leading from the front and empowering your team.

Fundamental to this are your existing relationships. In China, when Covid hit, I had already established myself as a respected leader with the team. I had arrived with a clear vision which I had been embedding within the team, I had a number of successes under my belt in the role and I had positive professional relationships with my colleagues. This certainly made it easier to say, "I don't have all the answers on this and need all of you to help me work out what is the best way through."

In fact, my team recognised that it took confidence to say, "I don't know." I took a more coaching approach to our discussions, using open questions with my team to encourage their ideas and problem-solving. For some of my team, this really helped them to develop. Some weren't used to being consult or listened to, so they grew in confidence as they suggested ideas and possible solutions.

As managers and leaders, we should all actively seek to offer such opportunities to colleagues to get the best out of them (of which more in the next chapter). In a professional context, many managers and leaders will need to give clear steers and instructions to their staff. But the really great managers and leaders will recognise when not to provide their teams with the solutions, to facilitate progress rather than drive it personally, leading through others.

This is often described as a *coaching* approach rather than a *directive* approach. And that's exactly what youth workers do. They know how to ask coaching questions to support a young person to find their answers. By doing so, you don't only help others to be better but also learn yourself.

Why not try this out yourself if you are a leader or manager who feels that they always have to come up with the answers? Maybe start with something low risk, so you don't feel too exposed. Try some open questions (avoid questions with yes-no answers) to get the creative juices of your colleagues flowing: What would you suggest as a possible solution? How might we look at this in a different way? If we saw this as a positive rather than a problem, what opportunities might the situation present?

As for competitors seeing your developmental approach as a weakness, my potential vulnerability in China became my strength. My team and I were able to come up with ideas about how to respond to emerging issues more creatively and more quickly than others. My colleagues running similar offices were coming to us for advice on how to prepare themselves.

The all-knowing parent

As a mother, I also know that this is a particularly tough one for parents. As we raise small children, we teach them how the world works. Teach them the basics of knowing right from wrong. But if parents continue to insist that they have all the answers, as they grow older our children see through that and begin to question this supposed omniscience. Certainly, many parents tell me that by the time their children are teenagers, they often refuse to listen to parental advice. As a parent, you are trying to protect them, but they don't want to listen to your solutions. So maybe trying a youth worker-type approach, a more coaching style and admitting we don't have all the answers can help us give young adults space to engage more positively with our parental support.

Paul: I worked with hundreds of children and young people before becoming a parent myself. You would be excused for thinking that youth workers can easily slip into the parent role. Not so. Very little about parenting is easy for anyone!

It is however true that many of the attributes in this book are transferable to parenting and that the two roles can complement each other, but do keep in mind that the context, interplay and relationships are very different. As a parent you have responsibility 24 hours a day 365 days a year. You will probably have a relationship with this child for the rest of your life and the child will depend on you and rebel against you in equal measure. Youth workers offer a different relationship to a child.

This attribute of *always learning* is particularly relevant to parenting. You are going to make mistakes as a parent. Own them. Learn from them. And move forward.

I remember being impressed by this quote from Frances Rodman: *"Just think how happy you would be if you lost everything you have right now and then got it back again."*
"That's so true," I thought. "We often don't appreciate what we have right now. I'm going to use that with my kids."

Soon after, my son Lee - then about 6 years old - was crying because he was ill and couldn't play out with his friends. My wife Julie and I both felt sorry for him and so I decided to go into his room and comfort him. I'll use the quote to help him cheer up I thought. I sat on his bed next to him and said, "Lee, if you lost everything you have right now, all your toys, your home, your pet puppy," but before I could finish the quote Lee screamed and was inconsolable. "Hang on!" I tried. I hadn't got to the most important part!

My wife ran into the room shouting and cross." What have you said to him?" I tried to explain. "Get out!" she shouted, as she comforted Lee.

I stood on the landing thinking: "Wow, that didn't go well. Maybe Lee just needed a hug." Always learning! Even we youth workers!

My good friend and fellow youth worker Greg Falola tells the story of when his daughter Coral, who was 15 at the time, was starting a relationship with a young lad. One evening Greg heard Coral coming in from a date and shouted Coral to come and talk to him. "What's up, Dad?" Coral asked. "Am I in trouble?"

"No, love," Greg replied smiling." You aren't in trouble. I just wanted to say that I have not been the parent of a child who was in a relationship before, and you are probably having a lot of feelings that you haven't experienced before. I just wanted to say, let's support each other through this."

Coral said:" Love you, Dad."

I shared with Greg that I admired his honesty and connection with his daughter. Greg said if you have never spoken about sex and relationships with your child, it comes as a bit awkward when you have to start the conversation in their teenage years. He recommends having comfortable and appropriate conversations about sex and relationships as they arise from an early age. Greg's one of those people I always learn from.

The gift of failure

What about failure? As we've just seen, we don't always get it right when we are learning. But fear of failure is often what holds people back from pursuing improvement. Not everything goes to plan and in fact it's a rich seam of learning, so embrace it when it happens and move forwards.

"We are all failures - at least the best of us are." J.M. Barrie

Paul: I once had three youth workers working with a group of teenagers in Cardiff. They wanted to try a new activity they had dreamt up between them. The group were told to bring a disguise in the next day. They called it *Disguised in Community*. (The acronym should have been a clue.)

It was a simple task. The group were asked to go out into Cardiff city centre and put on a disguise and the youth workers would find them. The thinking was they would dress as old people or homeless people and get a sense of what it was like to be a different person in society.

What could possibly go wrong? Well, everything! The whole exercise was called off after 20 minutes, never to be used again. The Cardiff community wasn't ready for groups of teenagers dressed for Halloween in mid-July. The worst case was two lads who were brought back to the centre by the police because their disguises were balaclavas, and their hiding place was a bank.

As youth workers we have many brilliant exercises for young people to learn from. A good youth worker will have around 50 puzzles, tasks and icebreakers they can pull out at any time. Many of which require no equipment or preparation. All these exercises start with a great idea, but most of them fail before they succeed. As long as nobody gets hurt it is part of the learning journey.

Speaking of exercises, here's one for you to try.

Exercise: How can you ensure that you continue to learn and develop?

Good youth workers support others to consider their own beliefs, values and actions. They also regularly do this themselves. Here's an exercise for you to try. Maybe with a friend (or 2), discuss the following questions. Focus on exploring different sides to the debate, as well as listening to the comments of your friends and seeking to understand where they come from.

Personal and Social Development Through Guided Reflection
Discussion 1:
Should you always confess to a friend if you have done something wrong?
Should the truth always come out?
Is it best not to know some things?
What is most important: to move on, forgiveness or truth in friendship?
What if anything, will you do differently? Will you be more forgiving of people? Will you forgive yourself? Will you seek advice?

Discussion 2:

Is it better to be forthright or diplomatic?

How would you like people to be with you?

In what situation might you be forthright? In what situation might you be diplomatic? Which do you normally favour?

What if anything, will you do differently? Will you be more open and honest? Will you take people's feelings more into account when talking? Will you respect both approaches?

Discussion 3:

Is it selfish to be rich?

What does it mean to be rich? Are you rich or poor?

Are you generous? What is important? Generosity? To look after you and yours? To be financially successful?

What if anything, will you do differently? Will you give more/less to good causes? Will you save and invest? Will you have a financial aim and plan?

Capture your reflections on the discussion

Was I considering different sides of the argument?

Note down two things that surprised you during the discussion:

1)

2)

Did I change my position during the discussion?

How would I approach future debates like this?

A final thought on continuous development: Question Everything

"I would rather have questions that can't be answered than answers that can't be questioned." Richard Feynman

Don't believe everything you read in this book! In fact, don't believe everything you read in any book. We are not saying you have to question everything all of the time - as you would go mad - but nothing should be immune to questioning however uncomfortable. A youth work approach to personal and social development asks challenging questions, not to achieve a conclusive answer, but to stimulate the thought process. To become the Best of Us, the best version of yourself, be curious and question the world around you.

Life is much simpler in black and white, right and wrong, good and bad, us and them. It is more difficult to look from another person's perspective. Getting people to question their acquired beliefs, values and actions may result in them coming to different conclusions. This is how we continue to improve, as communities and societies. We don't even know what questions and challenges will be posed in the years to come, so this mindset of being open to learning and challenging acquired beliefs is crucial for us to respond to the future.

Paul: I was once working with a group of young people in Manchester who were United supporters. I am a Liverpool fan. This made me the target of ridicule. Anything that interests young people is an opportunity to explore their thought process. I asked them a question. "Teams can buy and sell players. If Liverpool bought all your team's players and your club bought all Liverpool's players, who would you support?"

There was uproar at the question. I had been building my relationship with this group for some weeks, so it was only their respect for me which tempered their anger!

"I just want to know what you are actually supporting." I explained.

"The badge," one of the girls replied.

"Yes, the badge," they agreed.

"What if they change the badge?" I asked.

"It's the fans," one of the lads said." We support each other."

"No, it's the club's history," another lad said.

I thought it was worth probing a bit further, so I asked, "Football clubs are fundamentally businesses. Could you choose a different club to support?"

"Yes, we could but we don't want to," said some.

"No, you can never change your team," said others.

The session was a success, not because it achieved any answers but because it achieved calm and thought-provoking discussion. Football was very important to these young people, and it was not my intention to diminish their passion, but a youth work approach and blind loyalty are not good bedfellows.

Later that day, I asked them "Do you drop litter?" Most admitted they did. "Do you agree with littering? I asked. Off we went again.

An excellent youth worker and mentor of mine Jeane Lowe once said to me, "When everything appears grey, you are getting there."

We are going to have to learn to live with such uncertainty. Bias, propaganda, fake news and artificial imagery are becoming more prolific. Artificial Intelligence (AI) enables even greater manipulation of information. We cannot accept things at face value. Democracies rely on people making informed decisions. But to make an informed decision people need freedom of information, free speech and most importantly freedom of thought. Democracies need critical thinkers to survive.

"It is the mark of an educated mind to be able to entertain a thought without accepting it." Aristotle

Conclusion

None of us are the finished article and to become the best of ourselves, we need to be open to learn from others and question the world around us. Youth workers are always asking young people to consider how they can improve their behaviour, their relationships and their communities. It would be hypocritical if the youth workers were not continually looking to improve themselves too.

To be open to personal growth, to succeed in professional and personal contexts, we all need to learn to open ourselves up to continuous learning. No one got to the top in their field by settling for 'good enough.' The most successful people we have met walk around with a curiosity and a desire for continuous improvement.

Helpfully, you already are in the right place right here reading this book. You are on this learning experience, so let's take a further step along it now and consider something fundamental to becoming the best version of ourselves. Something that none of us can succeed without, but that all of us could do better at: *positive relationships*.

Attribute 2: Positive Relationships

"The good life is built with good relationships." Robert J. Waldinger

Research shows that strong social connections are linked to better sleep quality, immune function, better mental health, resilience and happiness. It's positive relationships, not money, intelligence or genetic make-up that are the key to lifelong happiness, so we should all be paying more attention to them.

By improving your relationships with others however, you will not just be more content, but more effective in your endeavours. Whether it's science, music, space travel or feats of engineering, most of humanity's greatest achievements would not have been possible without people working together to achieve them. But in fact, in many ways we neglect our relationships more now than ever before. Many people experience a breakdown in their relationship with themselves. Our screens take us away from true human interaction. Within our communities, many of us struggle to remember the names of our neighbours. But positive relationships are needed to underpin the success of any individual, any community, any society.

Think for a moment. What would it mean if people had better relationships? What would it mean in families? Businesses? Communities? Politics?

"If you want to go fast, go alone. If you want to go far, go with others."
African proverb

Paul: I've seen time and again in my work, that if a person has good, solid and healthy relationships, they won't go far wrong. Having worked with people who have suffered poverty, disability and serious illness, they can be far less damaged than people who have experienced issues with their relationships. Some of the most damaged people I've worked with have suffered at the hands of others or have suffered bereavement or marriage breakdown. Damaged relationships. And it's a vicious circle. As Pastor Rick Warren stated, "Hurt people, hurt people." Let's break that cycle.

Youth work is a noble art, and the effective practitioner has honed a range of skills which this book aims to share with you so that you may connect with people in a way that gets results. Underpinning youth work is a relentless focus on positive relationships. This is a key concept to grasp before we go any further, so let me share with you an insightful model of the different types of relationship.

The Relationships Framework

The Relationships Framework is a tool to help people to focus on improving their relationships as the fundamental underpinning for success across all areas of life.

The framework is divided into four levels and each level complements the others:

- Level 1: Relationship with self
- Level 2: Relationships with others
- Level 3: Supporting the relationships of others
- Level 4: Relationship with the community

Level 1: Relationship with self

The first level of the relationship framework is rooted in helping a person improve their relationship with themselves. The relationship with oneself is really the foundation of all external relationships. If a person doesn't have a positive relationship with themselves, they don't feel they're worthy of positive relationships with others, they cannot support the positive relationships of others and they will not form healthy attachments including with their community. A positive relationship with oneself is the building block for success at the next levels.

Level 2: Relationships with others

As youth workers we see that once a person has a positive relationship with themselves, we can start looking at helping them navigate the many relationships they need to build with their friends, family, teachers and colleagues. Improving at this level of the relationship framework means teaching people how to be empathetic to those around them and use the self-awareness, self-respect and self-esteem they gained from improving their relationships with themselves to be confident in their interactions with others. We work towards people enjoying better, healthier relationships with others. You will find a useful exercise for auditing your relationships with others below.

Level 3: Supporting the relationships of others

The relationships of the people around us are also crucial to our own happiness and success. Youth workers teach young people how to support others to develop positive relationships. This is where the relationship framework moves from self to something bigger and it's where we start to see the ripple effects of our hard work. People helping others, really leading change and having positive impact beyond themselves.

Level 4: Relationship with the community

People are social creatures and need a sense of belonging to a community. Many youth programmes work with people with the goal of them contributing positively to their communities and society more widely. This is where the magic can really happen when people make realisations about their worth through what they can contribute to their community.

Three important notes on relationships

1. **Your most important relationship is the relationship you have with yourself - and this impacts on all of your other**

relationships. We need positive self-esteem and good levels of confidence to have a healthy relationship with ourselves. However, many people have emotional baggage which impacts the way they view themselves and internalises a self-critical narrative which focuses on faults and flaws. This internal voice can remind us of every embarrassing moment that has happened in our lives and predicts failure in our endeavours. This can be debilitating in having a healthy relationship with yourself and left unchallenged it can also build insecurity to the extent that it can damage all your relationships in some way. It often results in looking to put people down or putting them on a pedestal - a superiority complex or, conversely, an inferiority complex.

2. **Relationships are on a spectrum**. There is a prevailing belief that relationships are either transactional or interpersonal. In a transactional relationship the focus is on <u>what you give</u> and <u>what you get</u>. In an interpersonal relationship the focus is on <u>you and I and how we care for each other</u>. It would be more accurate and helpful however to consider all relationships to be on a spectrum between transactional and interpersonal. That is not to say that that relationships can't be purely transactional or interpersonal, but generally there's a some of both going on at any one time.

3. **You can't win them all.** You can't have a good relationship with everyone, and this may be no fault of your own. You can choose who you like and who you want to spend time with and so can they. Perhaps they have for some reason taken against you. They don't

like your clothes, your accent or your attitude. Who knows. It is easier to get along with people if you can, so consider feedback, but be wary if you are compromising your values just to avoid conflict. Some people will dislike you because they think you don't speak your mind, and some will dislike you because you do! The most important relationship is the one with yourself, when that relationship is intact there is less of a need to seek the approval and acceptance of other people.

Working on Level 1: Building a more positive relationship with yourself through working on your self-esteem and confidence

Self-esteem and confidence are connected but different concepts. Self-esteem is appreciating and valuing yourself. This develops and changes with experience. Confidence is belief in your ability to do something. Both impact hugely on our relationships, especially our relationship with ourself.

Poor self-esteem means putting a lower value on yourself than other people (inferiority complex) or putting a higher value on yourself than other people (arrogance). Poor confidence means you are not aware of your ability. You think you can't do something when you can (under-confidence) or you think you can do something when you can't (over-confidence).

So ideally you are accurately aware of your ability (confident) and your ability does not impact on how you value yourself (self-esteem). This is how self-esteem and confidence interplay with each other. Affording yourself an unfluctuating value means you are more willing to try things (and laugh if they go wrong) and trying things is how you build your confidence. Confidence and self-esteem are different, but they do interact with each other.

(Before Einstein, people used to think that space and time were two different things but being a genius, he realised that the two concepts where actually one thing which he called *spacetime* and in 1921 he won the Nobel Prize for Physics. Now we have realised that two concepts - confidence and self-esteem - that people used to think of as the same are actually totally different. But to date we haven't heard a peep from the Nobel Prize committee. We live in hope. It's good we don't need external validation for our self-esteem!)

The confusion between the two concepts is further compounded when people use the term *self-confidence*. What does that mean? You are confident that you can do everything? So, for these purposes, *self-esteem* and *confidence* are two different things and there is no such thing as *self-confidence*!
One of the benefits of having great self-esteem is that you value yourself regardless of your abilities or disabilities and without comparison to other people. This means that you have no need to put people down. This is an excellent basis on which to build all your relationships.

Having great confidence means that you know of what you are capable and you are able to communicate this and who you are to people in the way you walk, the way you dress, and the way you talk. Confidence is a real advantage to whatever it is you wish to achieve. People are attracted to confident people.

Building your self-esteem

Although it may seem that those with positive self-esteem have been born with it, mental health experts and youth workers agree that it's perfectly possible to build your self-esteem. Remember self-esteem is an individual's attitude to themselves. Self-esteem impacts not just our mental health and our relationship with ourselves and others but can even impact our physical health too. Someone with high self-esteem can handle constructive criticism well and manage setbacks effectively without taking challenges as evidence of their own lack of worth.

Social media has been linked to negative impacts on self-esteem. In the heavily curated version of our lives presented on social media, it is hard not to compare yourself with the perfection you are seeing online from others. We need to remind ourselves - and indeed our children and teenagers who can be especially vulnerable to such pressure - that you are comparing yourself to a fantasy. Everyone has their challenges - just like you - but few of us rehearse that publicly on social media. Your self-esteem will be healthier if you focus on yourself, rather than compare yourself to the online personas of others.

Try these exercises:

1. We can be our own worst critics. To have a healthier relationship with yourself, catch your self-criticism, write it down. This brings awareness

about this negative self-talk. Examine what you have written and challenge it in the same way you would compassionately challenge a friend. Remind yourself that you are worthy.

2. Another approach recommended by phycologists for building self-esteem is use of positive affirmations. Daily affirmations can help you remind yourself of your self-worth. Try writing out a short positive sentence on a post-it note and sticking it to your bathroom mirror. It could be something like:

I am happy with my life

I am happy, healthy and loved

I am proud of myself and grateful for the things I have

Then at least once a day, look at yourself in the mirror and repeat the mantra aloud several times.

You. Are. Worth it.

Be your own best friend and everyone will benefit.

Where can we find confidence?

As mentioned, linked but different is confidence, which is about a belief in our ability to do something. We could have written a whole book on the subject of confidence. It is something we all admire in other people and something we want for ourselves. Confidence is a great asset.

It is often said that when two people go for a job, if one has skills and qualifications but little confidence and the other has few skills and qualifications but loads of confidence, the one with the confidence will get the role.

Let's start with a little puzzle. Which of these is the odd one out?
Money / Confidence / Authority / Fame

It's confidence. You can be given money, authority and fame, but no one can give you confidence. You have to find it for yourself. People can create an environment which is conducive to your finding confidence, or they can take steps to knock your confidence, but ultimately it is down to you how confident you are. So, we are sad to admit that in this section we can't give you confidence. What we can do however is explain what it is, what it certainly isn't, how to find it and how to help other people to find theirs.

Here is another piece of bad news. There is only one place in the entire world where you can build your confidence: outside of your comfort zone. For the purposes of building your confidence, there are only three states of mind which are relevant: your comfort zone, the stretch zone and the panic zone.

Please see the model on the next page in which the line indicates the potential for confidence building.

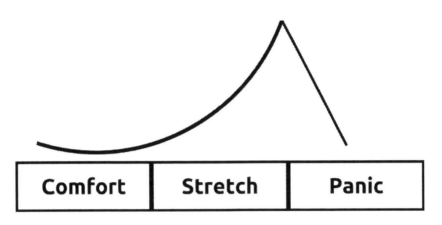

| Comfort | Stretch | Panic |

The comfort zone is when you are relaxed and not trying anything new, the stretch zone is where you are excited or nervous and with the right support, you have the chance to build your confidence, but the panic zone is where you have gone too far, you don't feel supported, and you want to get back to comfort as soon as possible. If you want to build your confidence, try something new, something a bit scary, but make sure you have support so that you don't go too far and end up in the panic zone.

The final piece of bad news is that building your confidence in one area doesn't mean you have built it in every area. Take a top sports person for example. They will have built up their confidence playing in front of dozens of people, then hundreds of people and now perhaps thousands of people. But ask them to make a speech and they might need to go back to dozens of people. They are out of their comfort zone. Learning to drive, asking someone out on a date, getting on the karaoke. All need work.

Confidence will not be universal in your life. It is contextual. The good news is that each time you move into your stretch zone you do become a little more used to being out of your comfort zone. Positive levels of confidence also contribute to positive self-esteem.

Moving to Level 2: Building Positive Relationships

Once we are in a good place in our relationship with ourself, we are better equipped to have positive relationships with other people.

As previously stated, people are drawn to confident people, but not over-confident or arrogant people (although watching arrogant people makes for good TV). But what else do we need to think about when developing our relationships with others? How about new relationships where you are starting from scratch? Let's take those in the world of work as an example.

Jo: Moving regularly around the world on diplomatic postings mean creating new relationships again and again. Arriving at a place where you know very few people can seem very daunting, but once you have a few new friends around you, it is a great boost to your resilience and positivity. Also in a new workplace, I often arrive knowing very few people, but to succeed in my role, I need strong and broad networks, so often need to "super-charge" the getting-to-know-you process! Some ideas on how to do this:

Step 1: Put yourself out there. Get one-to-one meetings scheduled with everyone you will work closely with. If you are leading big teams, go along to team meetings to get to know groups of people quickly.

Step 2: Be in listening mode. As well as presenting yourself to allow others to get to know you, in order to make connections, make sure you are asking questions and listen to the answers to really understand what is important for the other person. By understanding their needs and concerns, they will engage with you more.

Step 3: Collaborate. Offer help and ask for it too. Collaborating to work on common aims quickly deepens working relationships. Show gratitude for the work others have done for you. Gratitude shows respect and appreciation for others, which are important factors in positive working relationships.

"Trample the weak, hurdle the dead!" Skydiving t-shirt.

Unfortunately, popular culture can encourage combative, competitive behaviour in the workplace. Take popular reality TV programmes featuring sweary and aggressive successful businesspeople. These are caricatures, not reality. This is not how to achieve success. I have met Gordon Ramsey for example and can confirm he's totally lovely and charming. I've never met Lord Sugar, but it's easy to see that catchphrases like "You're fired!" make for better TV than "I can see you are struggling to meet expected performance levels. Let's get some coaching sorted out for you."

I've worked with some of the most successful businesspeople in the world and it is striking that so many of them are loved and adored by their colleagues and staff, held in high regard and respected. Sir Li Ka-shing - businessman extraordinaire known as "Superman" in Hong Kong and one of the wealthiest people in the world - whilst being very driven and a tough negotiator in important business negotiations, is friendly and engaging. One of the keys to his success is how he has inspired and motivated those around him. Consider these quotes of his from Forbes magazine in 2012:

"It doesn't matter how strong or capable you are; if you don't have a big heart, you will not succeed."

"To be a successful manager, attitude and ability are equally important ingredients. A leader inspires others to greatness. A boss dominates his subordinates and makes them feel small."

Those at the very top know the importance of relationships as key for success.

But what about when you have to work with someone you don't like very much? We all have to work with people we don't instinctively like or see eye to eye with from time to time. It can be hard to find the motivation to build a positive relationship with someone who you find difficult, with whom you have very little in common or someone you believe doesn't share the same values as you. But in the workplace, we must often work with people we wouldn't otherwise choose to be around. So how can we make such relationships successful?

Firstly, remember that you don't have to be friends with someone to have a good relationship, but *friendliness* goes a long way. Even if the other person seems cold or even hostile, responding with a friendly approach can diffuse tension and maybe start to thaw someone out who is just a bit of a cold fish. Some further steps will be particularly useful in these cases:

Step 4: Look beyond the person's behaviour. Try to understand why they are showing hostility or coldness. Put yourself in their shoes to try to figure out why your offer of friendly comradery is being rejected. Everyone has their own baggage. Maybe there's history of conflict between them and your predecessor. Maybe they see you as a competitor. How can you address this and move beyond it?

Step 5: Consider your own behaviour. Are you causing their hostility by something you are doing? Can you change the way you are approaching them to try to get a different reaction? Maybe you have different personality types that are prone to conflicting with each other. Consider getting insights ideally from someone who knows you both. In extreme cases, a bit of professional mediation can help people move on from conflict and work together.

For further advice, hang on for chapter 4 on conflict resolution!

Exercise: Relationship Audit

Before we go any further, let's do an audit of your current relationships.

Use the target picture below to plot out your key relationships. The middle of the target represents you. Plot the relationships in your life with those people closest to you nearer to the bullseye and those further away around the outer circles.

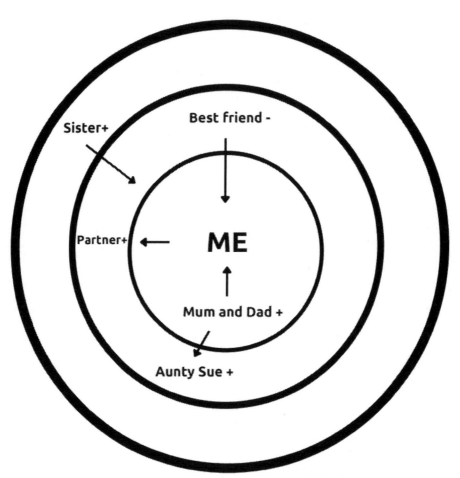

Then think about each relationship you have noted down in terms of whether it is a positive or a negative relationship by placing a + by the names of people where it's positive and a − by the names of the people where it is negative.

Now write against each person a direction arrow showing whether they are getting closer to you or further away over time, by drawing arrows pointing towards or away from the centre of the bullseye.

You can do this activity with a group or partner to share their observations. Write your thoughts down against the following questions. Don't overthink your answers. Just start writing and let it flow.

A. Do you have more positive or negative relationships?

B. Are you happy with where everyone is on the target?

C. Are there any aspects of your target which make you unhappy?

D. Are the positive relationships moving closer to you or further away?

E. Is there anything you would like to change about any of the relationships?

Note down **3 points of action** to take following this exercise to make change happen for the better in your relationships:

Action 1:

Action 2:

Action 3:

Focusing on Level 3: Supporting the relationships of others

There is a great deal of power in supporting the positive relationships of others. If you can see someone - maybe a family member or a colleague - struggling with their relationships, it might be that they need support with self-esteem so that they can repair their relationship with themself first.

Great youth workers - humble souls with good self-esteem - support young people to develop their relationships with themselves first by helping them working on their own self-esteem and confidence. As self-esteem and confidence are two different things there are two different methods to supporting their development. The way to support someone with their self-esteem is to affirm their worth with respect and affirmation. Since confidence development needs the person to explore their ability outside their comfort zone, they need encouragement and reassurance to do this.

People grow in their own time and sometimes it is two steps forward and one step back. When you are supporting others in this journey, as frustrating as it may be, it is important to let them choose their own development path. If you push them too hard, they are more likely to go into their panic zone, miss any learning and retreat to their comfort zone for a long time. Perhaps the rest of their lives. So let each person work at their own pace.

Other practical ways of supporting others to have good relationships

Paul: The historian Thomas Fuller once said, *"If you have one true friend, you have more than your share."* Well, if that's true, my wife Julie and I are incredibly blessed. We have a couple of best friends named Joanne and Rene Van den Bos. True friends are not in competition with you, they want to make your life the best it can be, and they help you to resolve problems whenever they can. They enjoy your company, and they advocate for you when you are not there.

Our children have all grown up together and all our relationships are precious. When their daughter Alex was planning her 21st birthday party they naturally invited us to attend. Unfortunately, it was also my brother Mark's 60th birthday on the same day. Mark was not having a party, but he did want to have a drink with me and Julie. This was a problem for us, as logistics meant we simply couldn't do both. After much handwringing, we shared our situation with Jo and Re who said to invite Mark and his family to Alex's party, so we could all have a drink with him. Given they didn't really know Mark and his family, the only reason they did this was to support our relationship with my brother and it was appreciated by all of us.

Helping people to relate to others

A friend of mine Joe Bradley works with young people with special educational needs to help them find employment. He was once working with a lad named Tommy who was 18 years old and had Down's syndrome. Tommy was a lovely, affectionate lad, but struggled to interact with people he didn't know, as he was really shy. Joe managed to secure Tommy a few weeks' work experience in a supermarket, helping customers pack their shopping. One day Tommy's mum called Joe and said Tommy was full of anxiety and didn't want to return to his placement. Joe paid Tommy a visit to find out what had happened. It turned out the store held a staff meeting each Friday and the manager had asked everyone to think of one way in which the store could be improved and bring it to the next meeting. Tommy did not have any suggestions to offer so he felt like he was letting everyone down.

Joe reassured Tommy (and his mum) that no one would be disappointed if he couldn't think of anything. Joe then asked Tommy what he liked about the store. Tommy said he just liked helping people and that friendly people used to smile at him when he helped pack their shopping. "Do you talk to them?" Joe asked. "Not really," Tommy replied. "I am too scared."

"What would you like to say to them if you weren't feeling shy," Joe encouraged. Tommy replied with a whole list of things he would like to say.

"Well, if you can't say it, maybe we could write it down and you could give it to them," suggested Joe.
Joe and Tommy's mum wrote down on slips of paper what Tommy would like to say to people. The next day when Tommy packed a customer's shopping, he would pop a slip of paper in the top. The slips said things like 'Thank you for smiling', 'You seem very kind', 'I enjoyed helping you'

and 'I hope people give you some love today.' Well, the customers adored it, and they loved Tommy! People would queue up to interact with Tommy even when other tills were free. Some people would go around twice just to have a chat! Over the following weeks Tommy came out of his shell and would smile and talk to people, but he carried on with his little slips of paper.

Naturally the store kept Tommy on after his placement and he became a highly valued staff member who knew many of the customers' names (Especially one customer named Jessica, but that's another story!) By helping Tommy improve his relationships, Joe had impacted positively on a whole community. And probably did wonders for the business of the supermarket too!

Conclusion

You may have spotted that we haven't gone into much detail on level 4 of the relationships framework here. That's coming up later in the book, so stay tuned!

This book and the insights shared within it will help you grow your relationships - with yourself and with others. By reading this book and acting on it, you will be part of the Making Relationships Great Again movement. Well maybe we'll get some better branding, but you get our point!

Positive relationships are the fundamental backbone of success in life whether personal or professional. Keep this key concept in mind as you progress through the book. Without the fundamentals of strong positive relationships in place, the rest of our advice will not be as effective, and you won't realise your goals. If you skipped through the exercises without reaching for your pen or stopping to ponder the challenges, it could be worth taking a few moments to go back and make a few notes. An investment in your relationships is never time wasted.

Once you've reflected on your learning in this chapter, it's time to move onto another key attribute that will serve you well in all aspects of your life but needs to be looked at afresh given the changes we see in our society: *effective communication.*

Attribute 3: Effective Communication

"Communication is the one most important skill you require for a successful life."
Catherine Pulsifer

Many hundreds of books have been written about the importance of effective communication. We are social creatures and so successful interaction with others is important for our survival and our ability to thrive. Here we want to focus on the aspects of communication that will best prepare us for success in the world with which we are currently faced and the technology-laden one that is emerging for the future.

Never in history have we communicated more than we do now. We all send messages, make calls, chat online, send emails, even thankfully still speak face to face occasionally! We are hyper-connected and communicating and being communicated with all of the time. Even while we sleep, our phones collect up the many messages and notifications that head our way during the night, so that as soon as we wake, we are blitzed with a wave of communication.

But even despite all this potential for effective communication, we still face the same old miscommunication problems (e.g. people feeling misunderstood or left out) as well as encountering whole new problems we didn't even know could exist until recently.

To offer some help, we do need to go back to some first principles here. First of all, communication isn't just <u>what you say</u>, it's <u>how you say it </u>and also <u>what is understood</u>.

Paul: Many of the youth work examples I've given already are underpinned by good communication. The very best youth workers I know can communicate well at all levels: with young people, to senior leaders, with police officers, teachers, with families and with their colleagues.

It has been said that 'communication is what lands' but that is an oversimplification. Effective communication is also contextual. In a fire, we need clear and concise instructions, but in other situations we don't just need information, we may need sensitivity. Great youth workers communicate with sensitivity.

There is an old joke in which an officer calls the Sergeant Major into his office and says: "Sergeant Major, Private Jackson's parents have been in a car crash and you need to inform him that his mother has died." The Sergeant Major salutes and marches out to the troops who are standing on parade and shouts out, "Jackson, your mother is dead." Jackson bursts in to tears. The officer overhears this and calls the Sergeant Major back up to his office. "That was awful, Sergeant Major. You showed no tact whatsoever. I have just heard that Jackson's father has also died. Go back down and inform him but this time be more tactful." The Sergeant Major salutes and returns to the parade. He shouts out "All those privates who have at least one parent still alive take one pace forward. JACKSON STAND STILL!"

We see effective communication isn't just what lands, it is about how it lands. It needs to be delivered selectively, with sensitivity, as well as clarity. Or failure and embarrassment will follow.

In 2011 when I was on holiday in Tenerife, I went to a bar to watch the England game. I went to the bar to order a round of drinks but with all the noise I had to lean over the counter and shout the order into the barman's ear. "Can I have 3 lagers and a fanta please?" The barman looked at me and said, "Are you John Lennon?"

"What?" I said totally confused.
"Are you John Lennon?" He repeated.

I didn't know what to make of this question. Was he asking me this because of my Liverpool accent? Was it happy hour and anyone claiming to be one of the Beatles got a free drink? Should I just say yes and see what happens? I decided that honesty was the best policy, especially as I would obviously be lying given that John Lennon died in 1980. Perhaps it was an honesty check for which I would be rewarded.

I leant forward again and shouted with absolute certainty. "I am not John Lennon."

The barman looked at me as if I was insane and said again, "Orange or lemon?"

Of course, embarrassment isn't even the worst outcome from poor communication. Major disagreements can have their roots in small misunderstandings. Conflict and war need excellent communicators to overcome divisions and mistrust.

Excellent communication is particularly important in teams and in large organisations. I have worked with organisations of all sizes and while it is easier for small organisations to communicate more effectively, I have never found an organisation which has totally cracked it.

Communication Mantras

Therefore, I introduce communication mantras into organisations I work with, so that as a leader my ideas around how I want us to communicate to each other and with our clients are clear and understood.

My current set of five communication mantras for my Vibe teams are:

1. You are only as good as your day off

Meaning that if you are off and people can't find anything or don't know what is meant to be happening you have not done your job.

2. Presume positive

Meaning if you hear that someone has said or done something, it is best to give them the benefit of the doubt and believe they had good intentions.

3. Take it to them

Meaning if you hear something you don't like, talk to the person directly rather than talk about them. This also applies to hearing something you really like. If you are impressed with someone, tell them.

4. What you permit you promote

Meaning if you don't challenge poor language or behaviour then you are allowing it to become engrained. Speak out against what is wrong.

5. Need to know

Meaning you don't need to know everything but trust us to share with you what you need. Too much information sometimes slows everything down and leads to organisations becoming inefficient. In terms of dealing with sensitive information, it's sometimes inappropriate to share.

I have found that having a small number of such communication mantras improves interpersonal interaction by sending a message across an organisation as to what is expected in our approach. Even if things don't go to plan, and people don't always keep to the mantras, at least there was a plan, and we can refer to the mantras as what people should be doing.

Let me unpack one of these comms mantras in a bit more detail. This final mantra *need to know* I got from my time in the army. In the military, the fewer people that know the detail of a sensitive plan can be better from an information management point of view but knowing who needs to know what and when is a work of art and takes serious consideration.

When I was younger, I was a corporal in the Territorial Army Parachute Regiment and did over 80 jumps with them. One day we were about to jump into Germany on exercise when the sergeant major (a huge man who nobody messed with named Bruce Cargill) called all the corporals together.

Bruce explained to us that the safe landing area (or dropzone/DZ) was very short. There was a forest, then a short piece of flat land (the DZ) and then some live electricity pylons. Bruce instructed, "The privates don't need to know, but if we are not out of the plane sharpish, the people at the back of the line will be landing on the pylons and almost certain death." (Now I also used to be an electrician, and I thought to myself that it was more like probable death than certain death, but I wasn't going to argue with Bruce as *that* would have been certain death.)

(I could mention here that paratroopers aren't as inclusive with their humour as youth workers - on which more in a later chapter - and it was often that as the line of jumpers was running towards the plane door, a new lad would have a hanky shoved in the top of his parachute kit by the man behind him, who would then shout, "Lad, your chute is hanging out!" The terrified lad would be running swept along with the rest of group towards the door unable to stop. He would scream to the dispatcher, "My chute is hang..." as the flow of bodies carried him out of the door.)

On the day, as we flew over Germany, everything was going to plan. We had been on the cramped plane for over two hours when the dispatcher indicated for us all to stand and prepare to jump. Above our heads running the full length of the plane ran a wire and on this wire were 30 hooks. One for each paratrooper. The military need to jump very low to the ground and there is no time to activate your chute, so this is done for you. Each parachute has a line which you must attach to the hook on the wire so that as you leave the plane the chute is pulled out for you. Hooking your parachute onto your hook is therefore an essential lifesaving act.

Unfortunately, on this occasion something had gone wrong. As we approached the extra short DZ, plane door open and ready, some of the hooks had moved and one guy (not me) in the middle of the group did not have a hook. He was screaming, "Who's got my hook, I've got no hook!" There was a spare hook further up the line, but to get it to him would mean everyone unhooking and sorting the mess out.

It was at this moment when the dispatcher shouted, "Ready!"

There was no way anyone wanted to unhook at this point, which was very bad news for the hookless guy. "Sergeant Major!" He screamed.

Bruce turned to face the group and told everyone to unhook. The mix up was being sorted, but we were losing valuable time above a short drop zone.

"Go!" Shouted the dispatcher. I had a hook, but I hadn't attached back onto it yet. The group pushed forward. I had the hook in my left hand and the line from my parachute in the other hand. I was trying to connect the two as I moved towards the door. I wasn't the only one and the stick moved slower than usual. "The pylons!" Came a shout from one of the corporals at the back to hurry us up. "The pylons are coming! The pylons are coming!" Another corporal shouted.

I felt the cold air from the open door on my face as I hooked in, just 2 seconds before I jumped out of the plane.

After landing, I gathered my parachute in and scrambled into a ditch where two younger soldiers were lying. I popped my head up to looked across the DZ to see if everyone made it. To my relief the last man out of the plane landed safely just short of any danger. I lay back down and turned to look at the young soldier beside me.

"Keep your head down corporal." One of the young soldiers said to me. "The pylons are coming."
These two thought that the pylons were the enemy we had been sent to fight. I realised that 'need to know' changes as the situation changes.

In fact, everything about communications is contextual and dynamic. None of the organisations I have worked with has mastered communication because it is not something you can master. The need, the tone, the message is continually changing and like a surfboard as soon as you think you have mastered it, you will fall off.

Don't beat yourself up therefore if you and your organisation are having some communication issues. Identify the problem and take steps to sort it out. But accept that this is only a short-term fix and better communication needs constant attention.

Effective communication is about trial and error, it is about adapting and gaining feedback. You may get there, but you can't relax at that point. What is needed is continual improvement. Get the message?

Comms Mantras Exercise (take 15 minutes)

Do you think your team or organisation could benefit from an improvement in its communications? Look back at the communication mantras for Vibe. Could you develop 5 such principles for your own organisation that if everyone held in the front of their minds would improve communications? What would they be?

1.

2.

3.

4.

5.

Now Jo speaks more than a handful of foreign languages, so should be able to offer us something on the topic of communication!

Jo: We live in a world where migration has created wonderfully mixed communities where we can benefit from different cultures and experiences. But of course, such a mixture of backgrounds brings challenges including communication challenges. Working overseas, I've worked in many multi-cultural teams, where there are additional obstacles to clear and sensitive communication.

Although I've always worked in offices where the main working language is English, working with a range of nationalities often means a range of mother tongues. Even where levels of English are very good, it's important to avoid idiomatic English. While you might think you are being perfectly clear asking someone if they are 'under the weather', this might not mean much to those for whom English is a second language.

How we communicate and what we talk about needs to be handled with extra sensitivity. In some cultures, discussing a person's age is deeply insulting, but asking why someone has not yet had a child is perfectly fine! Context and relationships are also key here, balanced with an understanding of the cultural norms. If in doubt, get advice and proceed with caution.

Communication in the digital age

I also want to concentrate here on how we communicate effectively in the digital age. In an age too of mobility, we are increasingly living further away from family and friends, maybe relying on a family WhatsApp group to share news and keep in touch, rather than picking up the phone or taking the time to meet up face to face. In the workplace too, with many of us working attached to our screens, even days working from within the office can just be a series of video calls.

Technology unequivocally helps us stay connected. But does it make us stay better connected? Not necessarily. Some of the **key challenges for communicating well in a digital world** – and some suggested solutions - are:

1. **Information overload**: With too many notifications on our phones, overflowing email inboxes, messages and channels filled with endless information, it's unsurprising that few workers nowadays feel that they can stay on top of their communications.

But how to address this? Can you walk across the room to speak to someone to avoid another message or email that might get lost in this tsunami of information? Maybe someone isn't replying to your quick message, not because they disagree or are being unhelpful. Maybe they just need to discuss the issue face to face to make a decision. Can you give them that opportunity?

What's more, our attention spans are shrinking thanks to the way digital communications condition our brains. So messages need to be concise to stand any chance of cutting through the noise. If you have to write your message, have you done so in a way that gives it a chance in this busy, unfocused digital world?

2. **Misunderstandings:** It is said that 80% of interpersonal communication is non-verbal. Imagine therefore everything we are missing out on when we receive an email or message. We can't see the sender's expressions, hear their tone of voice nor see their body language. In the absence of that 80% of information, there's a real risk of misinterpretation.

One key way we can try to tackle this in the digital world is to keep your camera on in a video call. This allows for more non-verbal information to accompany your words and you can show you are engaged and listening when others are speaking. By smiling and nodding, you can show your agreement and encourage others. And of course, keep your eyes peeled for the non-verbal signals of others on the call.

How about using emojis? Whilst I'm not suggesting going overboard with this, indicating your support for a comment during meetings with a thumbs up or celebrating a success a teammate posts in a chat with a suitable gif is one of those ways we can go beyond mere words in the digital world. This might not work in a very serious high-level meeting, but would be much appreciated in many other contexts, so make sure you read the virtual room appropriately!

3. **Lack of human interaction:** Messaging and emailing - however well-drafted - still leave lot to be desired especially around important or sensitive issues. Let me tell you a story about the problems it can cause.

When Covid broke out, most of us were sent to work from home. During this time one of my team who I normally saw every day at work found herself being harassed by another colleague. We had been chatting via short messages every day, but she didn't mention the situation on there. Instead, she had sent me an email making a complaint about the harassment. Unfortunately, the attachments got caught by the email filters and I never received the message. A few weeks of what I thought was perfectly normal messaging later, I finally picked up the phone to speak to her directly about something. It was clear immediately that she was unhappy with me. Since I hadn't replied to her email, she concluded that I was ignoring the situation or even perhaps taking the side of the other person. We were thankfully able to figure out the lost connection quickly and I reassured her by immediately following up.

But how long might this have gone on if I hadn't picked up the phone? Already it went on for a few weeks. Too many. I had thought that we were communicating well by exchanging short messages each day, but if fact, she was totally frustrated that I wasn't responding to her email. From the short messages, I couldn't tell that.

So this is a plea for something of a digital detox of your communications. Pick up the phone to your colleague, drop by for a cuppa with your mum, arrange a day out with a friend. The only way to check if your communication is effective is to really check - and double check - if and how it is landing. Sometimes it's impossible to do without being in person.

Paul: Before we get into a final comms exercise, I wanted to share a further key lesson for me in terms of communications as a leader: <u>sometimes you need to recognise that you aren't the person who needs to communicate your message</u>. Let me tell you another story.

I am not of any political persuasion. I do however take voting very seriously. Most political parties seem to have some merit in their core aims, but how these aims are interpreted can vary tremendously. I like to look at their leaders and their manifestos before making my decision. Having said that, it is a strange system which is akin to choosing a restaurant knowing that you are going to have to eat everything on the menu. Anyway, I have had the opportunity to work with politicians of various denominations to develop the country's youth sector. As such I agreed to be youth policy adviser to David Cameron.

In 2006 a 15-year-old boy named Jessie James was murdered in Moss Side in Manchester. A local youth worker Geoff Thompson called me and said, "Paul, it is going to go off here. People are furious with the way the police have handled this murder. Can you get David Cameron to come here and listen to them? I fear there is going to be a riot."

At that time David Cameron was Leader of the Opposition, but the idea was that he could visit as a key public figure who could listen to the community. I passed the message on, and I ended up being the go-between. A community meeting was arranged in Moss Side for David to attend. On the day of the event, I wasn't planning to attend and was having breakfast and getting the kids ready for school with my wife Julie who was busy ironing school uniforms.

My phone went. It was Conservative HQ." Paul, David wants you to attend with him." The Moss Side community were angry at the police so David would not have any close protection offices. Perhaps because he knew I was a black belt in karate or perhaps because he didn't really know what to expect, he had decided he wanted me at his side.

But I would have to rearrange my whole day and I heard myself say, "I'm not sure I can get there on time." The voice said," David and his driver will be at your door in about ten minutes to pick you up." I looked around the room. There were toys, breakfast dishes and clothes on the floor. I looked at Julie who had frozen mid-ironing and had a look of outrage and horror in her eyes. She shook her head and mouthed an expletive. I said, "I will meet him at the end of the road."

About an hour later David Cameron and I walked through the streets of Moss Side together. As we arrived at the community centre, we were welcomed by the community leaders and shown into a side room to meet Jessie's mother and hear her heartbreaking story. She told us the awful story of how someone had knocked on her door and told her that her son had been shot. She had run along the road, but the police stopped her approaching Jessie's body, since it was a crime scene.

We sat and talked for some time and then David and I were escorted into a community hall where there were two seats on the stage. I sat next to

David and the head of the community centre introduced him. The hall was packed with about 150 people. There was absolute silence. I looked around at their faces. They looked sad, hurt, scared and angry.

David stood up and thanked everyone for attending. I felt ill at ease and thought I hope he gets this right or we are likely to be lynched. David had not prepared a speech and he started with a statement." If I become Prime Minister, I will focus on supporting people from areas like this."

A man immediately stood up and shouted, "What do you mean areas like this?" A second man jumped to his feet and shouted," It's people like you, saying 'places like this' that give places like this a bad name." Several more people stood and shouted. I was about to stand and ask for calm. (It did occur to me however that a scouser shouting, "Calm down, calm down!" in Manchester may just add fuel to the fire.)

Just in time a man at the front stood up and turned to face the crowd. "Give the man a chance," he said. "We invited him here, give him a chance to talk." The crowd settled back down. The man turned to face David and said, "Please continue."

In youth work this is called *using the room*. Someone acting on your behalf can afford you some authority as sometimes you may not be the best person to communicate a particular message. For example, if you need people to be quiet you don't start shouting for it, you can ask someone else in the room, "Can you please get me their attention?"

David continued, "I really didn't mean to cause any offence, by areas like this I mean areas of high unemployment, poverty and crime." He spoke a little more and then said he was there to listen and learn. He asked people what they thought the issues and solutions were. We stayed for over an hour and when we left the atmosphere was very different.

My takeaway from this experience was that when you have a message, ensure you listen first, be clear what you want people to feel, think and do. Finally consider this: perhaps someone else will be better placed to communicate your message for you.

Better Communications Exercise

There are many aspects of effective communication. We've touched upon a few key reflections from our experiences here, but it's a subject which has already been the subject of many thousands of books, articles and blogs. It's clear that it's something fundamental to all of us and something on which we all need to keep working. Here's an exercise to help you on that journey.

Paul: I was once on a flight from Manchester UK to the US. One of the plane's engines developed a serious fault and the pilot, sounding genuinely rattled, told us he needed to shut down the engine, drop most of the fuel over the sea and make a complicated emergency landing back at Manchester airport. I became a bit anxious, especially when one of the stewardesses started weeping and praying. On our approach to

Manchester, the pilot came over the intercom with the ominous message, "Good luck, everyone."

I knew there was a real chance of us crash landing in the next 20 minutes. You, the reader, know that I survived of course, but me at the time thought I could well be facing my end. Those 20 minutes were very poignant. I could only communicate with the people on the plane. But they were facing the same existential threat that I was. Many of them were praying, some of them were meditating, but none of them seemed to want to talk.

I felt the need to connect. I felt the need to communicate. Not really with the strangers around me, but with those people who had played a significant part in my life and who were blissfully unaware and safe on the ground. I thought of four people back home who I wanted to talk to and what I wanted to say. When I survived, I made sure I had those conversations.

Reflecting on it afterwards, it turned out that they were four very different conversations that started with:
1. A question
2. An apology
3. Gratitude
4. Forgiveness

The exercise (take 10 minutes):

Think of each of the four types of conversations above.

Is there a question you would like to ask someone?

Is there an apology you would like to make?

Would you like to thank someone for something?

Is there someone you would like to forgive?

Decide what you would like to say and to whom. Write these down. Are you going to make any of these conversations real? Would they be more impactful, more meaningful as a hand-written letter or said in person?

They would be powerful examples of communication.

Conclusion

Effective communication is something that underpins good youth work as well as a great deal of success (or lack of it) in our personal and professional lives. How to communicate effectively is a topic of endless challenge and opportunity. We hope that this chapter has given you a few more tools to help develop more effective communications with a particular focus on some of the challenges that are facing us in the modern world.

Poor communication can create misunderstanding and conflict, whereas great communication can build powerful and positive relationships, find solutions and bring people, communities and nations together. Our next chapter focuses on *conflict resolution* - a key area where youth workers have to put their communication skills to regular use. Let's have a look at just how they do that now and what you can learn from it.

Attribute 4: Conflict Resolution

"The quality of our lives depends not on whether or not we have conflicts, but on how we respond to them." Thomas Crum

The quote above underlines the inevitability of conflict. This could be quite disheartening, but Crum also indicates that conflict does not have to be damaging. It can actually be beneficial. It would be impossible to make progress as individuals or as a society if everyone agreed on everything. Conflicting ideas, beliefs and values help us to explore things from different perspectives and gain new insights. At this level conflict is healthy and progressive, but we all know that conflicting ideas can escalate into serious disagreements and arguments between people, even between nations.

In recent years, we have seen conflict escalate to war in Europe and tension in the middle east turn into war. Back home in the UK, we saw summer riots break out in 2024, stirring up tensions between and within communities. In order to tackle hostile environments, we need more peacemakers, more people who can resolve, even prevent conflict. In many ways this is a youth worker's bread and butter.

Paul: Vibe - the youth organisation I currently head up - has been providing youth work support to music festivals. Festival organisers know that they need security guards and police officers, but enlightened ones also know that youth workers offer them something different. Something very powerful.

At a recent festival our youth workers were called over to an incident at the main gate. A large group of young people were in a standoff with a small group of police officers. The police wanted to search the young people before they entered the site. Our youth workers spoke to the police. The police needed to check for drugs and weapons and were about to call for reinforcements. Knowing that this would escalate the situation, our youth workers asked the police to hold off while they spoke to the young people.

The young people explained that they were convinced that the police were going to plant drugs on them, arrest them, take them away and beat them up. To avoid what moments before had seemed like an inevitable conflict, the youth workers offered to stand and watch each search, which – because both sides trusted the youth workers - satisfied both sides. Tension was managed and the youth workers had proven that they were worth their weight in gold once again.

Conflict Escalation

Conflict can escalate – sometimes quickly – and as it does, it can be harder to resolve. From starting out looking for a win-win solution, people can move to a win-lose position trying to beat their opponent. If this doesn't work, they might get to a lose-lose approach where both parties are so invested that they are prepared to destroy their own position in order to stop the other. Understanding the mindset of the parties involved in the conflict in relation to this helps services, including youth workers, to work out appropriate intervention strategies.

People who are descending further and further into conflict can benefit from some timely impartial external intervention or mediation.

But it is not just young people who descend into conflict.

Paul: As I experienced one evening a few years back, when on a London train heading back up to Liverpool. The train was delayed, which at least allowed me to go grab some humous and carrots from M&S, but when they announced the train was ready for boarding, there was a mad rush as hundreds of weary passengers dashed to their seats. As I boarded the train it was clear that total confusion reigned. There had been no time to download the seat reservations on to the electronic seat indicators, so all the seats were indicated as available.

A female voice came over the intercom." My name is Betty and I am your train manager for this evening's journey. The computerised seat allocation system is not in operation, so no seats are reserved. Please sit anywhere. We are sorry for any inconvenience."

It was like when the music had stopped in a game of musical chairs, everyone grabbed the nearest seat. Winning, I even I managed to grab a nearby table seat.

Opposite me was a well-suited middle-aged businessman who looked like he had had a full day. He hugged a briefcase in his arms. It was clear to me that he was waiting for the train to pull out so that he could get his laptop or papers out and continue working. Not me. I had had enough for one day, so settling back I took my coat off and got the carrots and humous out of my bag. Plunging a huge carrot into the creamy dip, I munched away. Oh, the bliss.

Just before we pulled out another flustered and tired looking businessman jumped on the train. He'd obviously been running late and must have been surprised that the train was still there. He walked up and down the coach holding and checking his ticket. Eventually he stopped and said to Briefcase-man sitting opposite me. "You're in my seat."

Briefcase-man explained the train manager's announcement. "I am just following instructions. Just sit anywhere."

Late-man looked around the train and saw all the seats were taken. "I don't care," he said." You are sitting in my seat and I need it."

"Well, I'm sorry," said Briefcase-man." But this is no longer your seat, and I am following the train manager's instructions."

At this point someone with good youth worker skills could have helped find a win-win solution with a timely intervention. Perhaps asking them what the problem was - the act of giving an explanation can sometimes take some of the heat out of a situation. Or perhaps give up their own seat - embarrassing them into finding a solution. Or perhaps offering to go find the train manager.

I didn't do any of these things. To my shame. It could have just as easily been me in Late-man's seat. But on this occasion, this youth worker was far too shattered and besides, couldn't talk due to a mouth full of carrot and humous.

The conflict looked set to descend and descend it did. The problem stopped being about the seat and started being the other person. "Listen, pal," said Late-man. "That's my seat and if you don't move, you will have the worst journey ever."

The situation had clearly moved to win-lose. "Do what you must," shrugged Briefcase-man.

As the train pulled away, Late-man seemingly started to back off but then turned around walking back towards Briefcase-man. Wondering what was going to happen next, I slowly dipped my carrot in my humous and before

89

placing it in my mouth, used it as a secret pointer to warn Briefcase-man that his adversary was returning.

Late-man walked straight passed, but smacked Briefcase-man on the back of the head with his elbow as he went by. Briefcase-man's head whipped forward and his face grimaced. Late-man walked a few more steps up the train and then again, he turned and started walking back toward briefcase man who growled, "You dare do that again!"

"I told you, you would have a bad journey," yelled Late-man and as he went passed, knocking Briefcase-man's head with his elbow. Briefcase-man span around and punched Late-man on the backside.

"Ow! Oh my God! Ow! He's punched my arse!" Howled Late-man as if he had been shot.

He turned and grabbed the other man by the collar." Get out of that chair!" As the two men were wrestling, I picked up my humous pot to move it out of harm's way.

"Get off, get off! You'll get us both thrown off the bloody train!" Shouted Briefcase-man.

"I don't care!" Screamed Late-man. We had now moved to lose-lose. The time for mediation and compromise had passed and the situation now required policing. Other passengers started to intervene, physically trying to separate the two men. With what now looked like a rugby scrum in the middle of the carriage, I decided there was no way I could help, as adding another body to the mix could only make things worse.

"STOP THIS!" Came the loud, commanding voice of authority. It was Betty, the train manager. A fearsome looking woman who wouldn't have looked out of place as a matron in a 1950s hospital sitcom. "Stop this now!" She said with a menacing lower-toned growl in her voice. Gradually the passengers on the outside of the scrum withdrew to their seats. Leaving the two men in the middle who slowly let go of each other.

"Behave yourselves!" Instructed Betty with a fearsome look on her face. "There are children on this train. Behave yourselves," she repeated several times pointing at various people, including me. I was indignant to have been told off, given I hadn't done anything, but I thought the best course of action was to just take it and I lowered my eyes and my carrot to the table.

"What's all this about?" Betty demanded.

"He's got my seat!" Insisted Late-man trying to sound righteous but sounding more like a sulky child.

"There are no allocated seats," snapped Betty giving him a verbal clip around the ear. "Give him this seat," Betty said to Briefcase-man. Briefcase-man complied with the instruction and stood up. Late-man sat down in the seat with a smug satisfaction as if he had just won the world chess championship. But his contentment was short lived when Betty told

Briefcase-man to come with her to a seat in first class. Peace descended and our train journey continued into the night.

When Betty came back into the carriage to check people's tickets, I heard a woman with broad Liverpool accent say: "Excuse me, love. Whose arse do I have to punch to get upgraded?" The whole carriage, including Betty, broke into laughter.

Conflict is best tackled early before it escalates. This is exactly what good youth workers are there to do (whether they are knackered and eating humous or not). Youth services are often used as early intervention to resolve issues before them become entrenched, but where a conflict has gone too far, policing and (youth) justice services might well need to be involved.

Keep calm and carry on

Jo: As someone who has worked as a diplomat, you'd hope I have some useful insights to offer in this area of conflict resolution.

Firstly, an example of how not to do it. Not long ago, I had the honour of working on The King and Queen's State Visit to France. After months of hard work, the day was finally here that my team and I would be hosting Their Majesties at a large concert and cultural showcase with over 1200 invited guests. We were all very tense, as we knew that the stakes were high and the tasks ahead of us complex. We knew that due to security concerns, we would have to turn away any guests who could not provide appropriate photo ID. We had singers with demanding riders. We had companies with last minute dramas.

My team was quite stressed, but as I did the morning briefing, having just previously written the first draft of this chapter with Paul, I was channelling my inner youth worker and had the solution. "Whatever happens, whatever anyone says, keep calm and polite," I instructed with what I hoped was a calming smile. "However stressful the situation, however irate the person in front of you, being polite and calm will de-escalate the situation."

The event was a huge success, if the most intense afternoon of my life. (I can say that as I gave birth on a morning.) The crowds, the police, the King and Queen. It was a lot for all of us, but my team kept their cool, politely diffused any tension and managed any difficult individuals professionally.

As Their Majesties left, I could hear one man's raised voice, insisting to be let into a restricted area with one of my team looking panicked. As I went over to help resolve the issue, the man's irritation refocused on me. I immediately lost my cool. It had been a tough day, week, month…or two! Going against all the sound advice I had given my team, I snapped at him insisting there was no way I could let him into the restricted area for security reasons. As our grumpy exchange escalated, he said his name. Ah…the chairman of the company who had sponsored the whole event. It seemed that one of my team had tried to be helpful by storing his luggage for him. Now he wanted to retrieve it urgently as he had a train to catch, but it had been placed in our secure area. I'm still hoping that when we next meet, he doesn't remember me. Maybe next time, I'll remember to follow my own advice.

"Intellectuals solve problems, geniuses prevent them." Albert Einstein

Resolving conflict is often a diplomatic pursuit, but in fact *preventing* conflict is more a diplomat's bread and butter.

Developing personal relationships

In my first diplomatic posting, I was sent out to Brussels to represent the UK in European negotiations. Despite the polemics trotted out in some corners of the media, negotiations in Brussels were rarely big clashes of ideals with countries throwing around their vetoes. But lower-level tensions were common. Proposals set forth by the European Commission were rarely wholeheartedly welcomed in their entirety by all the Member States - numbering 15 countries when I first started this work and growing to 25 by the time I left - and so negotiating to find agreement was my main daily task in my area of responsibility - education and youth policy. A key foundation for finding agreements and building alliances was the development of personal relationships with my opposite numbers on the Education Committee.

Whilst specialists on each file would be sent out from capitals for the meetings, those of us on the Education Committee that were based in Brussels remained the same no matter the specific area of negotiation. This allowed us to smooth the negotiations by knowing the characters, knowing their preferences and tactics and above all, having existing friendly relations which would bear weight when put under pressure by conflicting national positions. It was often much better if there was a conflict between countries' positions, to pick up the phone to a friendly contact and discuss it informally than to argue across the negotiation table.

This is another aspect of resolving or preventing conflict: picking the right time and place to make the intervention. I often found that in public, in our case at the large European Council negotiation table, people might feel that they had to take an uncompromising position, but in a one-to-one environment, it was difficult to be obstinate when they had a person in front of them asking for some help to find a way through.

Another aspect of dealing with conflict, is to work with mutual allies. As mentioned in the communications chapter, you aren't always the right person to give the message. This is often true in the context of conflicts. If you have tension in a relationship, it might be best to ask an ally to interceded on your behalf first. Someone who both parties trust - as in Paul's example with the music festival search - can help create a bridge between the two sides. This is often the case in international conflicts - a third country trusted by both sides will mediate peace talks. I often used this approach in Brussels. Sometimes the message simply wouldn't be heard if it was delivered by the Brits, but sometimes if a third country made the point, it would be viewed differently.

Often conflict resolution does simply take quite a lot of patience. During the UK Presidency of the EU in 2005 (which came shortly after the 2004

EU Enlargement - itself a key geopolitical example of conflict resolution since this was designed to reunite the continent after the fall of the Berlin Wall), I was chairing a working group of the now 25 Member States represented on the Council's Education Committee. The UK government was keen to get agreement on the current negotiation to demonstrate its success in the chair, so the pressure was on to get everyone to sign up. I had been working on the agreement for months and had - I thought - lined everyone up behind the text on the table during the penultimate meeting.

"We object." A hand went up as I asked for the vote. It was the representative of one of the smaller countries who had recently joined the EU. Until now they had been quiet during the discussions. I didn't think they cared much, but it seems their instructions had just taken a while to arrive and now in what I had thought was my moment of glory, they stuck an ugly spanner in my beautiful work.

I should explain that although the committee voting worked on a weighted majority system with larger countries like ourselves, Germany and France holding the majority of the decision-making power, we always sought to have a board consensus in our agreements, since it made for more loyal implementation as well as better working relationships between the countries. If a proposal already had the backing of the three big countries, you only needed the votes of a few of the other 22 members, but bullying through agreements doesn't make for good international relations, so certainly in the groups where I worked, we always sought to get everyone on board.

Still, the smaller Member States tended to understand the limits of their influence and so negotiated accordingly. This particular country with only a few votes at their disposal couldn't stop the agreement, but it would leave a very bad taste in everyone's mouth if I pressed on ignoring their objections, especially since this was a new EU member. It would have been unprecedented. I reluctantly stopped the vote. What followed was frantic work over the next few weeks, in part to gently help the representative to understand that the amount of influence they really had (limited, so they needed to be a bit more pragmatic) as well as tying to address their key concerns. With each change to the text, I had to ensure I wasn't losing support from other countries, so getting everyone on board took a fair bit of to-ing and fro-ing. I tried not to be resentful, but patience hasn't ever been one of my superpowers.

Finally in time for the committee's last meeting of the Presidency, I'd secured this 25th vote of support without losing anyone else's along the way. But more than that. For the next negotiation, I was the one needing to build alliances with the smaller Member States, and guess who came to my aid!

Conflict Resolution exercise

All current conflicts have a past, a present and a future.

Think of a conflict in your personal or work life that can be explored with the following questions.

We suggest taking about 5 minutes per section.

Past

What happened that signified the start of this conflict?

What fuelled this conflict in the run up to the start?

How has this conflict developed?

Is there anything you would like to change about what has happened?

Present

Why is the conflict continuing?

How do you feel when you think of this conflict?

Do you have a role in continuing the conflict?

Do you or anyone else benefit in any way from keeping this conflict going?

What is this conflict doing to you?

Future

If you stay as you are now, how do you see the conflict developing?

Can you see any benefits to resolving this conflict?

What different approaches could you take that may resolve the conflict?

What would you like to happen?

Finally

What are you going to do?

Where and when is the best time to do this?

Who else can help you with this?

Parenting

Paul: As a parent, you can't avoid conflict, so you certainly get plenty of practice at handling it!

One day I took my children Lee and Siobhan round to my friend's house to play with his two children. Not long after I arrived some other parents arrived with their three children.

The adults sat in the kitchen talking while the seven children went upstairs and played noisily together. I found the noise reassuring as the children were all under 10 and one thing more worrying than a house full of noisy kids is a house full of quiet kids.

After a while Siobhan came into the kitchen and said that Lee had pushed her over and hurt her arm. I gave her arm a rub and told her to go and tell Lee that I wanted to talk to him. She went back upstairs and a few moments later Lee appeared in the kitchen. I felt the eyes of the other parents watching me to see how I dealt with this. "Lee, did you push Siobhan over?"

"No, dad," said Lee the picture of innocence.

I gave him a serious look and said, "If I find out that you are pushing your sister there will be trouble. Now go and play." Lee ran off and to my mind the matter was settled.

The other parents had stopped talking and they were staring at me. One of the mums asked in disbelief, "That's it?"

"Well yes," I replied. "Siobhan has been heard and Lee has been told. They are all playing together again."

"Oh wow," she said. "I would have got far more involved with lectures, threats, sanctions and punishments. I have a lot to learn from you." The others agreed.

I was surprised at their approval for my minimalist methodology but looking back I do think many modern parents can be too involved in their children's lives. Taking responsibility for conflict resolution, education, entertainment, nutrition, happiness, relationships etc. It is exhausting. Of course, you have to care for your children but there is a balance to be struck. Sometimes less is more, creating a space for your children to grow and learn how to deal with these things for themselves, allowing you space to enjoy adult life. Then when you do get involved it has more significance.

I have taken a lot of youth work skills into my parenting. I have been a youth worker, and I have been a parent, but I'll admit, it is easier being a youth worker!

Conclusion

Youth workers need this key attribute as young people are often in conflict with themselves, with their parents, with authority figures. De-escalating tension can benefit us all, in everything from international negotiations to managing our own families.

We often ignore conflicts as we don't understand how to deal with them effectively or we cause a conflict to worsen by not addressing it. With the approaches outlined above, hopefully you feel you have more tools available to you to effectively bring people together, address tensions and de-escalate conflict in your relationships and those of others, making you more likely to achieve your goals and maybe also achieve more win-win situations, benefitting everyone.

The realities of life mean that conflict is never too far away however, which even with the greatest conflict resolution skills can seem exhausting. This takes us to our next attribute, which youth workers need to be successful: *resilience.*

Attribute 5: Resilience

In recent years the world has become a tough place to be. The 24-7 news reels constantly scream out upsetting headlines. We often feel overwhelmed by our busy lives. Each generation goes through more relationship break-ups than the one before. We, our teams, systems and organisations all struggled through Covid. We all need to battle through the stresses of work. War drags on in Europe and the Middle East. Many people are having to tighten their belts in the changing economic context.

So, we are all in need of resilience. In spades. You'll be glad to know that since youth workers need a lot of resilience, whilst also building that of others, they have a lot of advice to offer on this topic. They must continually deal with some extremely challenging situations – and personalities – day after day, week after week, year after year. (For frankly a fraction of the thanks or remuneration that they deserve, but that's for another time.)

A story of inspiring resilience

Paul: I had been working with a group of youth workers to coach ex-athletes from the *Dame Kelly Holmes Trust* for some time and we came to know them well. The topic of the day was: *How to support the development of resilience in young people.* We explored what resilience is and how it can be born out of failure and adversity. This really resonated with the athletes, many of whom had had to face defeat, loss and injury in order to ultimately achieve success.

We had created an exercise that would help the athletes explore adversity for themselves, giving the athletes 10 tasks to do in two hours. This included jigsaws, bridge-building, treasure hunts etc. They were naturally competitive and set about planning their time and resources.

But there was a catch. We gave everyone an envelope with an extra challenge inside (youth workers love this one): being blindfolded, not being allowed to talk, not using their arms or legs. One of the athletes, Anna Turney as a para-athlete was already paralysed from the waist down, so we had debated about whether it was fair to give her one of our created obstacles. In the end, we decided to give her an envelope anyway, adding a blindfold as an additional test.

Most of the athletes struggled with their new disability and some literally sat quietly in the corner unable to figure out a way through the tasks. They were people who are used to being very able-bodied – the peak of physical performance – and some of them really struggled when that was taken away. The group was heading towards a disastrous failure. The youth work staff didn't mind, as they knew it would be a learning opportunity either way. But the athletes seemed gutted to be failing.

Then what happened next was pretty amazing. Anna took control. Since she was blindfolded, she started asking people what was happening, then started providing clear leadership for the struggling group: making plans, solving problems, encouraging others, using humour and encouraged the team to an amazing success.

All of the athletes and the youth worked staff learned from Anna that day. Since she was used to additional challenges, the "blindness" didn't faze her. Her resilience was higher, as she practiced overcoming obstacles each and every day.

Clearly a big part of resilience building is overcoming adversity, so next time an unwelcome challenge comes your way, try to welcome it as an opportunity to get stronger. Perhaps too, a big part of resilience is focusing on what you have and not what you never had or what you have lost. There's little doubt that life will continue to throw challenges our way, so you'll have plenty of opportunity to practise this!

The Risks of Resilience Culture

Resilience has become one of those buzz words in recent years. But what does it actually mean? Resilience is the capacity to adapt quickly and successfully to difficult challenges, quickly returning to a positive state. It can help us manage stress and avoid anxiety and depression. It is increasingly cited on job specifications and is measured in performance appraisals.

To us however, the advice often given sounds a bit too much like the dreaded "English stiff upper lip." In previous generations, we were encouraged to bottle up our emotions. We were told that the best way to deal with whatever was thrown at us was to "Keep Calm and Carry On." And yes, to a certain extent, sure. If you were to start complaining loudly every time your boss asked you to do something that you didn't like, your glittering career might well be cut short well before it had ever begun.

Today however we have a much better understanding of the importance of emotional well-being and how to maintain positive mental health through opening up about how we are feeling. Developing resilience can protect your mental health. But for us, we see a real risk that this "you need to be resilient" message can be unhelpful. If we avoid facing up to difficulties confronting us or put off getting the help we need for too long, this becomes a destructive concept. If we dare not talk about mental health challenges because we think it will mean we will be passed over for exciting projects or a promotion, it creates a negative and unsupportive work culture. Our society is moving away from leaders who are cut-throat tough-nuts and is looking for those who have more authenticity and compassion.

This is particularly true for the next generation of workers. Positive mental health is important for all of us, but anyone working with Generation Z will know that they are much more aware of their emotional well-being than those who have gone before. So those of us parenting them, working with them, managing and leading them, need to be very conscious of this and engage with them on the topic with authentic support.

Defined as those born between 1997 – 2012, Generation Z have very different priorities to their millennial elders (never mind those of us who can remember there only being three TV channels). They bring their whole self to work and demand that the organisation supports their wellbeing. So simply telling them to "toughen up" just won't cut it.

Our advice on the tricky topic of resilience is:

    1) focus on developing your own resilience

    2) understand "it's ok not to be ok"

    3) support others to develop resilience with compassion and understanding, especially for those who are finding things tough.

So here – with compassionate challenge – we offer three supportive suggestions for boosting your resilience.

Resilience Exercise 1: Purpose

Psychologists have repeatedly found that people who have a strong sense of purpose experience more resilience. Use these questions to reflect on your own sense of purpose. Note your answers and discuss them with someone else if you can.

1. What gets you out of bed in the morning?

2. When do you feel most alive?

3. What does being successful mean to you?

4. What do you wish you were doing in your life that you aren't?

5. How might you change things to enable you to do the things that would give you more sense of purpose? Are there things you need to stop doing?

6. What did you do today that made a difference to someone else's life?

7. Imagine you are on your deathbed decades into the future. What advice would you give to your current self?

Resilience Exercise 2: Kindness

Research shows that happiness and resilience are boosted by performing acts of kindness, such as helping others. Now this is something that makes a great deal of difference for youth workers. The reason why they can press on with what might sometimes seem like impossible tasks is the great feeling of satisfaction they get from helping young people. Try some of these activities:

- Do a random act of kindness e.g. pay for a stranger's morning coffee tomorrow or give up your seat on a crowded bus.
- Sign up for some volunteering. This might be anything from a one-off activity like going on a local litter pick to volunteering regularly with an organisation that needs support.
- Be extra kind to the people you spend your time with tomorrow.

Note down how you feel after undertaking these activities and how other people reacted to what you did.

Resilience Exercise 3: Gratitude

People who practice gratitude are found to have boosted levels of resilience. Some ideas for developing this tool as part of your resilience armour:

- **Put a piece of paper or notebook by your bed and every day for the next week, before you go to sleep, write down 2-3 things that you were grateful for that day. At the end of the week, re-read what you have written and note down how you feel.**

- Write a thank you letter to someone you wish to show gratitude to. This could be for something they did for you or just something about the way they are that you really appreciate.

- Tell your family and friends what you really appreciate about them.

Challenges to Resilience: Handling Crisis

"The ability to stay calm under pressure and manage your emotions has a direct link to your performance." Travis Bradberry

Let's now look at when our resilience is really tested: moments of crisis. Youth workers are always dealing with crisis. Sometimes these are real crises, sometimes they are just perceived as a crisis by a young person or a parent. In either case, being calm and confident is a tremendous asset. Easily said? The more that you experience a crisis, the easier it gets, but it also helps to have some simple rules.

We seem to be facing crisis after crisis in the modern world so don't worry about having a lack of experience, as mentioned, unfortunately life will provide! Take heart in the knowledge that the more crises you survive, the more capable you will become. It is also worth remembering that whatever the situation you are currently facing, if you reframe it as a learning opportunity, you'll immediately feel a bit better about it. Your current situation is exactly what you need as preparation for next year's real crisis!

So here are four golden rules that we have found useful in a crisis, which have proven effective again and again for youth workers.

Rule No. 1: Be prepared.

There is a certain amount of planning that you can do for a crisis. Start by brainstorming a few possible crises that could pop up in your life or your work.

For youth workers, they have training in the type of difficult issues with which young people might present: a bereavement, being excluded from school, having problems with the police. Whilst experience will of course make us more competent at dealing with such problems, training and planning also help. You wouldn't expect a pilot to be put in charge of an aircraft without some training in what to do if an engine packs up. In such moments, pilots also use checklists to focus the mind and ensure that key issues aren't missed.

Jo: I've worked on several crisis situations with the Foreign Office and training and preparation has been incredibly important. Teams are trained up at home and around the world to be ready to deal with a plane crash, a tsunami, a coup, whatever it might be. We rehearse scenarios and develop processes and procedures to ensure we have structures to support our people and their decision-making. Having a process to follow is also helpful in the first few minutes when stress might mean that emotions can run high. Being prepared and knowing what your first few actions should be can focus the mind and avoid panic.

Try this exercise to do some simple planning around a crisis that could arise in your life:

1. Describe the crisis situation you might be faced with.

2. Identify two things (if any) you can do now to mitigate the risk of the problem occurring.

3. If this crisis broke out, what would the first three things be that you'd need to do?

4. Who would you need to help you with this? Have you got their contact details handy (saved in your phone)?

5. What resources do you need to have ready just in case?

Rule No. 2: You can't be fully prepared!

No matter what your preparation and training, life will throw up challenges and crises that you haven't considered. If in a crisis, you can only deploy the rules you have been given, you will not have the flexibility you need to respond to complex situations. Robots can follow rules, but do not (yet) have the problem-solving skills and creativity of human beings. To be effectively decisive though we need to practice self-awareness and self-control.

This is where character education comes to the fore. You will be able to deal with any crisis far better if you know who you are and what you stand for. By investing in your personal and social development every day you will be better grounded and ready for the challenges you will face in life even – and especially – at times of crisis.

Personal development requires you to explore your beliefs, values and actions. This means questioning the rules which are being applied by your employers, your religion, your family, your community etc. Not to be awkward and obstinate, but so you can choose to adopt them, amend them or reject them.

Not all these institutions will welcome your open mindedness! But unless you explore for yourself the rules and norms around you, you will not develop a healthy framework to guide your life. You are unlikely to have time in an emotional situation to start questioning the rules and norms, but if you have prepared yourself with your considered beliefs and values, your actions will flow from that and allow you to make clear decisions in any difficult situation.

Invest in your personal and social development now to develop your character (for example by working though this book!) because you need to know who you are before the crisis starts. You will need to take charge (at least of yourself if not of others) and you don't want to have to start questioning yourself and your context at that point.

Rule No. 3: Focus on what you know, what you don't know and what decisions you need to make.

Information is at a premium in a crisis, it can be the difference between winning and losing, survival or death. But there is an optimal time to make a decision. Ask yourself: do I need to make a decision now? If so, make it with the information you have. Too often leaders suffer from *analysis paralysis* meaning they are waiting for a moment of certainty before acting. That moment of certainty may not arrive any time soon or at all. If you really need to make a decision, make it.

To make a good decision, you also need to *focus on what you know*. This doesn't just refer to the information available to you, it also means controlling your mind so you avoid both catastrophising (thinking the worst) and optimism bias (assuming everything will be fine).

Let's take a look at this. If you went into work and your boss said: "I need to see you in my office in 10 minutes," what would you think? Something bad has happened? That you are in trouble? That your boss is cross? Or "Oh good something great has happened and maybe I am going to get a pay rise"? Most people lean towards the negative. This is because there is an evolutionally benefit to thinking negatively. Those humans who anticipated danger were more likely to survive. If you imagine there is a tiger behind every bush, you will be more prepared when one is actually there.

The problem is that continually anticipating the worst is stressful and does not necessarily make for good decisions in the modern world. By applying the *focus on what you know* rule to the boss wanting to see you, all that you actually know is that the boss wants to see you. The rest is in your mind. You could ask your colleagues if they know anything so that you can get prepared but be careful that your mind doesn't create a tiger.

If your child is late home, what you know is: your child is late home. Catastrophising can lead to panic, which can make your response inefficient or inappropriate. Do you need to make a decision to do something? Then make your decision and do it.

In a crisis situation, you might need to consider different possible scenarios that may play out and prepare for them, but importantly: without panicking about the additional difficulties that may come along. Always remain clear-eyed about what you know and what you don't know. What is happening and what has not yet happened – and might never happen. You need a clear picture of reality to cope with and manage a crisis successfully. If you need more information, seek it.

Jo: This was important to me in China when we started to get news about a new virus that was sweeping the country. I needed to educate myself about the risks of the virus to be able to make the best decisions for my team and my family. I reached out to a public health expert I knew and got a briefing on what the medical and public health community knew about the virus, which helped me be calm about the (minimal) risk to my young child, but mindful and able to make plans for the older members of my team and family, as it was clear from early on that they were the ones most at risk. Knowledge is power and it helped me make the right decisions at the right time.

Paul: I have made decisions which have proven effective, and I have made decisions which have gone wrong. When they go wrong, I consoled myself in the knowledge that you can only make a decision with the information you have at the time. Looking back at the times I have been most disappointed in myself are the times when a decision was needed and I failed to make one, or at least not a timely one.

Some years back Simon Weston and I had been working all morning in Liverpool at the *Weston Spirit* office looking at how we could boost the charity's profile. Simon had a certain amount of fame, but he was rightfully concerned that it was all on his shoulders. If we could get some more well-known people to show some support, we could do a lot more for young people. At lunch time I went out of the office down to my favourite shop on Lime Street to grab some carrots and hummus for lunch (I'm a creature of habit). On my way back, as I turned the corner, I bumped into a man coming the other way.

"Sorry," we both said and sidestepped each other before we continued on our way. Two steps later I realised who it was and stopped dead in my tracks. It was one of Britain's finest comedians: Billy Connolly. I had the idea to run back to him and say "Billy, can you spare us a few minutes? There is someone I would like you to meet." Who knows where a meeting between Simon Weston and Billy Connolly could lead? Perhaps he would offer to do a gig for *Weston Spirit* or just become an advocate or offer to meet some of the young people. But then I thought: he must get approached all the time and I don't want to be 'another pest' and he is probably on his way somewhere important to do something important with someone important.

"No," I thought. "How great would it be for the whole team if I walked back into the office with my carrots, humous and Billy Connolly?" I decided to go for it! I turned and ran back, but it was too late. He had disappeared into the crowd. I scanned around, but he was nowhere to be seen.

Perhaps he would have said yes or perhaps he would have said no, but we will never know. My hesitation had killed the opportunity, and I have lived with that ever since. Now I know this wasn't a crisis (it's not like he had knocked the carrots and hummus out of my hand), but it is an example of the mistake of not making a decision when one was needed. I would be fine with having decided to turn around or walk on but being rooted to the spot was a mistake and a big regret that I still think about.

Rule No. 4: Identify the people who need your attention and those who can help you

My mother used to work on a supermarket cheese counter. She put in for a promotion and during the interview her supervisor asked her the question, "Can you name the most important person in our branch?" My mother thought for a moment and replied, "The most important person in every branch is the customer." She got the role.

It is crucial to be aware of who the most important people are in any situation, especially in a crisis. There are over 8 billion people on the planet. You can't cater for them all. In any situation you need to ask yourself, "Who do I want to focus on at this moment?"

During a crisis this may change as circumstances change. If your office is on fire, your focus will be on the people in the building. Once people are out, your focus may change to the injured, then family of the injured, then your main stakeholders, then key customers, then back to your team for example.

In today's age of the 24-hour news cycle, the media might also need your attention. In a professional crisis (or even in a personal one if you are very unlucky), you might need to deal with media scrutiny. The media are very powerful and can be scary if you are facing a crisis but remember that their power is spread across the public. So as a leader think carefully about the public messaging and how to get that across. This might include talking one to one with some key people. If you phone the 10 most important people to your situation or organisation and let them know what is really going on for example, that can help counter the narrative of a media attack. (Have you got those key people listed with their contact details?)

Remember that you may not be the best person to do the communication or indeed other tasks. you might need to delegate.

Paul: Greg Falola once said to me as a leader, you shouldn't have any problems. If someone brings you a problem, your job is to find out whose it is and give it back to them!

"Surround yourself with great people; delegate authority; get out of the way." Ronald Reagan, 40th president of the United States

I don't know if you will think that what I am about to say is a good thing or a bad thing but in a crisis, you will not be able to do everything yourself. The good news is that unless you have been marooned on a desert island you won't have to. Identify those who can help you. Find support, ask for help, distribute the work.

Let me give you an example of how a team can be valuable in a crisis. We had not long arrived at the residential youth centre which was located deep in the Lake District and miles from the nearest village. There were four members of staff and myself and we were just getting to know this group of twenty two 16-year-olds from one of the tougher areas of Manchester.

Energy was high and the group's excitement was palpable. We never really knew what to expect on these residentials, but I had every confidence in my team. My second in command was Tony Smith who had led his own courses on many occasions. The other staff were more junior but were fast learners.

We were in the midst of the first discussion session, when one of the lads – Baz – suddenly stood up and started to scream for help, terrified. His legs were marching on the spot and his arms were grasping upwards, as if climbing.

I asked the screaming lad directly, "What's happened, Baz?" He stopped screaming but carried on his panicked climb.

"Who knows Baz?" I asked. Two young lads raised their hands. "You two stay with me. Tony, take the rest of the group outside and do something with them."

"What is going on?" I asked his friends. There had been nothing his medical return, but the friends explained to me that they had been at a party a few weeks earlier and someone had spiked Baz's drink. He had become obsessed with the film *Jacob's Ladder* and when he freaked out like this, he believed he was on a ladder that was descending into hell.

I asked one of the younger members of my team to replace Tony outside, so he could come in and talk to me. I told Tony that I needed him to take Baz to the nearest hospital. "Take one of the junior staff members and one of his friends with you." I advised.

We manage to talk Baz into the car, and I felt a sense of relief as Tony drove away. The remaining staff and the rest of the group sat down to lunch a little shaken. We can restart the course after the lunch I thought. I congratulated the staff and the young people for how they had helped me deal with the situation. It had helped bond everyone together really quickly.

I was deep into my cheesy beans on toast when the door flew open. An elderly woman ran in shouting, "Please help me!"

I stood up." What's happened?" It turned out that she had been walking when her husband had collapsed. He was on the floor in the woods about half a mile away from the centre. The elderly woman had run to the nearest building, which happened to be our centre, and she was clearly out of breath and obviously in shock.

All our staff know first aid, but there were only three of us left. I didn't want to send a staff member to deal with the situation alone, but I didn't want to leave one staff member alone with 20 young people. Especially given how this day was going – there was likely to be a helicopter crash into the building at any moment!

One of the teenage girls on the course said:" I know first aid."
"Repeat that." I said hardly daring to believe my own ears.
"I know first aid," she said again and I looked at her like she was a god-send. I decided to use the young people to help us deal with the situation. Anything we had planned couldn't be as good a team building opportunity as this anyway.

"Right," I said to a junior staff member." You take the girl who knows first aid and go and check on the man." I instructed the remaining member of staff to call an ambulance.

"You two." I pointed at two of the group." Sit with the lady and get her a cup of tea. The rest of you, we are going to form a line of sight from the centre to the casualty, so that when the ambulance gets here, they will find the man without any difficulty." The man had had a heart attack, but within 40 minutes he was under the care of an ambulance crew. Which considering his location was impressive.

Later that week the woman called back into the centre with some chocolates and a card. She told us that her husband had survived and was doing really well. Baz never returned to the course and sadly whilst he had been stabilised that day, he would continue to have mental health issues.

Considering that this was a training course for young people, I (as always) learnt loads in leading this programme. (Including not to choose cheesy beans in a crisis, because if you get called away, they have to go in the bin. Choose carrots and humous every time.) In a crisis you are rarely on your own and if you want people to act responsibly, give them responsibility. They also need clear guidance though, which brings us onto rule 5.

Rule No. 5: People need clear leadership

In a crisis, people often want to help, they just need some leadership. If you are in a leadership role during a crisis, step up and perform accordingly or step aside. If you are going to be the leader, be the leader. Show confidence and delegate. Without apology and with clarity.

A crisis needs a style of leadership that is different to leadership in everyday life. Most people know this, and they are willing to accept it.

Churchill was a fantastic war time leader, but if you are going to lead in both war and peace you will need to be able to adapt your style. In a crisis you need to be confident, forthright and clear, but in everyday life you need to be more collaborative, compromising and developmental. Remember Churchill lost the election immediately after the war.

Also recognise that leadership and management are different things. In a crisis you need both though not necessarily from the same person. Leadership is about people, relationships, vision and emotions. They also need to make sure that someone is doing the managing. Management is about processes, systems, policy and resources. There are far more great managers than great leaders. This is why we all have a lot to learn from youth workers. Youth workers are leaders, and in a crisis, we need great leadership.

Paul: I have taken many a first aid course but the best one I ever did was run by Sergeant Graham Clarke in the army. It wasn't even the medical side which was so impressive. I learned that even if I was in a civilian situation, I could still instruct people and take a lead. Just step into it, state why you are taking the lead and start distributing jobs. "Right, we are going to save this woman's life. I need you to call an ambulance and let me know when they are on their way. I need you two to go into that supermarket and get the first aider and a first aid kit. I need you to kneel with her and let me know if she has any problems breathing. I need you to put pressure on that cut." Etc etc.

(Quick tip – When leading in a situation like this don't point at people with a single finger, in can feel aggressive. Use a straight hand with all fingers and thumb straight and pointing in the same direction.)

Dealing with an imminent threat

Paul: Ok, let me give you an example of when I faced a very difficult situation that called on my crisis leadership skills. One evening I was at the train station with my wife Julie, we were waiting to travel into the city centre to meet some friends for a drink. The weather was cold and damp and there was nobody else around. A message flashed up on the board to say all the trains had been cancelled. We turned to walk off the platform and down the path back to the main road.

It was dimly lit, but at the end of the path we could see a group of five people standing by a car. As we got closer, I could see there were four men and a woman. One of the men was holding the woman by the neck, pushing her against the car. I felt a surge of adrenaline, as I believe bullies must be challenged and the sooner the better.

I didn't need to explore my beliefs around this in the moment – I knew my values. Walking past and letting this happen would be against everything I believe. Russia's President Putin stated that "big fish eat little fish." Meaning that if you are strong, you get to do what you like and call the shots. We only live with any freedom now because brave people in the past have stood against tyranny, organised crime, intimidation etc. I am clear in my beliefs around this so action naturally flows from that.

The group hadn't noticed us and as we were only a few steps away, the man who had hold of the woman drew his fist back to punch her in the face.

"Hey!" I shouted so loud I shocked myself. All five of them were startled. They all looked at me and Julie. The man lowered his fist and said, "Who the f*ck are you?"

I looked at the young woman and around the group at the four men. It seemed to me that they all knew each other, but I had no idea what was really going on. I didn't know the cause, but I didn't need to know about the cause. I wanted to protect the woman from the blow, but I did not want to put my wife in danger. Being trained in karate gave me a level of confidence in a one-on-one situation and as a youth worker it wasn't my first time breaking up a fight. But this isn't a Hollywood movie, and a one-against-four fight would have an inevitable outcome. (I am doing Julie a disservice here as she would have definitely got stuck in. But that was another reason I didn't want to fight!)

"I said who the f*ck are you?" The man demanded, shouting now.

"We are going to stop this before it gets out of hand." I said firmly. I didn't answer the man. I looked over his shoulder to the tallest of the group and said to him: "You're his mate and I need you to talk him down."

To my everlasting relief, he put his hand on the angry man's shoulder and said, "Come on. Come away." As they started speaking to each other, I turned to the two men on my right. "You two need to take her somewhere safe away from here." Perhaps because their buddy had done as I had instructed, they agreed. I turned to the young woman who looked like a rabbit in the headlights and asked her, "Are you happy to go with them?" She nodded. The tall man and the angry man continued to talk while the three of them went off down the road. Julie and I set off in the opposite direction and continued with our evening. Peace had broken out, but if I hadn't intervened, who knows what the outcome may have been.

There are no guarantees of success, but I have found that by following the above rules, you will have the best chance of finding the bit of luck you will need.

Crisis Exercise – Look back over the story above and see if you can see where each of the 5 rules were applied.

Rule 1: Be prepared.

Rule 2: You can never be fully prepared, so know yourself.

Rule 3: What do you know and need to know to make a decision?

Rule 4: Who is your focus?

Rule 5: Clear leadership.

Answers –

Rule 1: Be prepared. I have training in both youth work mediation and martial arts – though the karate taught me that in this situation, mediation was needed!

Rule 2: You can never be fully prepared, so know yourself. I have developed a strong belief that bullies need to be challenged and know that this is action I will take.

Rule 3: What do you know and need to know to make a decision? I knew the young woman was in danger. I didn't know what had caused this situation and I didn't need to know. I needed to know that the woman was happy to go with the two men to let that happen.

Rule 4: Who is your focus? The young woman was about to be beaten up so she was initially my focus, but my wife was also a priority. The angry man was surrounded by people who knew him and so I could draw on their help to manage the situation.

Rule 5: Clear leadership. I stated what needed to happen in a way that no one could disagree and then I gave out instructions.

Conclusion

We are all in need of resilience. Resilience isn't about a stiff upper lip but is about developing an ability to ride the storms of life without letting them beat you.

Whether you are thinking about long-term resilience or resilience in acute moments of need like a crisis, the character development journey that you are undertaking whilst working through this book will be of great help.

Life will certainly provide you with plenty of challenges to practice your resilience, so it is worth taking some time to work through the exercises here and indeed review them every year or as your circumstances change.

Another attribute that will ensure you can face the storms of life's voyage is explored more in our next chapter on *humour*. If you can laugh at yourself and your situation, it is easier to keep calm and carry on. Let's take a closer look at how humour is a tool we all need to reach for regularly.

Attribute 6: Humour

Humour is important to human beings. Many, if not most people, have felt the stresses and strains of modern life taking a toll on their mental health. Holding on to a sense of humour can be one of the most powerful ways to stay healthy and to support the people around us. Humour is a powerful thing: it can be a sword and shield, a force for good or evil. This chapter explores humour and how to use it to best effect in your life.

In this chapter we will explore

- Where does humour reside?
- What is it?
- Who has it?
- How can it be used to best effect?
- Why is it important?
- When should you use it?

Where does humour reside?

Paul: The day my father died family and friends gathered at my mother's house. Arrangements needed to be made but people just wanted to be together and especially they wanted to be there for my mum who seemed to be in a daze having lost the only man she had ever loved and to whom she was happily married for over 56 years. There was a sombre, sad and respectful atmosphere in the house as the family gathered in near silence. My dad had been ill for some months, but it still came a shock to us all when he died.

Given this is a chapter on humour, I bet you're now hoping we don't write a chapter on depression! I have started a chapter on humour with one of the saddest days of my life to illustrate that humour is irrepressible and a fundamental part of human nature. We were quiet for most of that day. But as time went on, we started to talk of my dad's life, laughing at his many crazy capers. I remember going from tears of laughter to tears and back again within minutes.

Humour is omnipresent. It may be laying low for a short while, but it is there. Ready to be activated at the first opportunity.

Not only is humour ubiquitous, it is also powerful. It can win friends and influence people. But some people find it easier to access, appreciate and utilise it more than others. Great youth workers can deploy humour to engage someone, disuse tension and make a connection. All things many of us need to do in our day to day lives.

Humour, when used correctly, can be a special power. But like fame, beauty and wealth it can make - or break – people.

If you don't believe us, ask Gerald Ratner who destroyed his jewellery empire with a single joke that some of his products were crap. Or Chris Rock who got hit at the 2022 Oscars after joking about Will Smith's wife. Humour is omnipresent and powerful. We need to understand it.

What is humour?

To start with let us clarify that humour is not the same thing as being funny.

Humour is a state of mind, a mode, disposition. Funny is being witty. Being funny can be humorous, but being of good humour doesn't mean you are necessarily great at telling jokes. If you feel in good humour, you are more likely to say or do something witty (at least intentionally). But most importantly, if you are in good humour, you are more likely to see the funny side of things. Equally, if you are in a foul mood, nothing is going to make you laugh. Nobody wants to feel depressed, angry, stressed or scared. There are theories that humour came about in humans as an antidote to all these things.

Research and common-sense states that people work better and are more productive when they feel better about themselves and their colleagues. That is not to say they are all cracking jokes and rolling about laughing all the time. Just that it is better if they are in a positive state of mind. Being ready to see the funny side of something as soon as the situation allows can be very helpful.

Take a moment to consider: How is your state of mind today? How is the humour in your team? How is your energy contributing to it?

Who has it?

Paul: A few years back I got sponsored to perform stand-up comedy for 10 minutes. Wow! That was a challenge. Hats off to all the professional comedians out there. There were seven of us all doing it for charity. We got trained by a comedian named Stephanie Davies from an organisation named *Laughology*. She gave us tips about how to walk on, how to hold the mike and how to deal with the audience. But what we were going to say was down to us as individuals. We trained for a few weeks and there was a great camaraderie amongst the seven of us. Some people seemed naturally funny, and others didn't seem to have any idea what to say.

The big night came around. I remember walking out on to the stage at the student union. Hundreds of people were looking at me and they only had one question on their faces: Are you going to make us laugh? Although I was really nervous, I went on in good humour and once I got my first laugh, I loved it, and my ten minutes flew by.

A woman named Jill went on after me. She struggled and only got a few titters, but as she came off the stage, I remembered her beaming face. As she passed me, she said, "I was awful, but I loved it!" It was at that moment

I realised that not everyone has the ability to be funny, but everyone can be in good humour.

Another member of the group got himself all worked up and just before he went on, he collapsed and taken to hospital with a suspected heart attack! Whatever you are facing, you will do better if you can stay light-hearted!

How can we use humour to best effect?

Here are a couple of my favourite jokes. See if you can see what they have in common.

Joke No1

A man joins a silent order of monks, where they can only speak once every five years.

Five years go by, and the head monk calls him in.

"Having kept to your vow of silence for the past 5 years, this is your opportunity to speak."

The monk says, "Can I have some sugar on my porridge of a morning?"

This is sorted.

Another 5 years go by, and the head monk calls him in again.

"What would you like to say?"

The monk says, "Can I have an extra pillow?"

This is sorted.

A further 5 years go by, and the head monk calls him in again.

"What would you like to say?"

The monk says, "Can I have a thicker curtain?"

This is sorted.

Another 5 years go by, and the head monk calls him in again. "What would you like to say?"

The monk says, "I have decided to leave."

"Well," says the head monk. "I can't say that I'm sorry. You've done nothing but moan since you got here."

Joke No2

A man goes into a bar and asks for 4 pints of beer.

The bartender pours the beer, and the man takes all four to his table and drinks them one by one.

The next Sunday, he does exactly the same.

On the following Sunday when the man comes into the bar and orders 4 pints, the bartender says. "Why don't you buy your drinks one at a time? That way they won't go flat."

The man says, "Oh, what it is, is I have 3 brothers and every Sunday we used to go the bar and have a drink together. They have all emigrated now, but we still all go the bar on a Sunday and have a drink like we are all still together."

"Oh, that's lovely," says the bartender.

The following Sunday the man comes into the bar but only orders 3 pints. The barman is saddened and says to the man, "Please have these on me and I am sorry for your loss."

"What do you mean?" Asks the man.

"Has one of your brothers died?" Asks the bartender.

"No," says the man. "That's me. I am on antibiotics."

What do the two jokes have in common? Well, they are both inclusive. They are not making any individual or group the butt of the joke. They are not belittling any race, gender or religion.

Inclusive humour can be a real asset

In April 2001, Sky TV had a community initiative named *Reach for the Sky* which aimed to inspire and motivate young people. It consisted of a number of workshops based on Sky's different channels (news, sport, the arts etc). It was truly inspiring for thousands of young people.

I was leading on the project for the organisation I started with my friend Simon Weston *Weston Spirit*. One issue we had however was that Sky wanted us to work in Belfast. Weston Spirit had never worked in Belfast before and given that both Simon and I had a military background, we weren't sure that our offer would be well received by the local community. We took the advice of two local youth workers David Gardiner and Paul McKinstry who recommended we met with leaders on both sides of The Troubles. In effect, to get their blessing. We did this with a trip to the Falls and Shankill roads. I admit to being on edge at the start of these visits and I know Simon felt the same, but we need not have worried. We found everyone in Belfast to be very welcoming. It was three years after the signing of the Good Friday Agreement and people wanted some normality and of course they wanted the best for their young people. We got the approval we needed.

We didn't want to bring across a team of youth workers, as we felt the local youth workers had more lived experience with the young people of Belfast.

So, we formed a team of local youth workers and set about training them. David and Paul warned us that the local youth workers may resent us turning up out of the blue. They said we could expect comments such as, "Where were you when the bombs were going off?" In reality though no one could say that to Simon Weston, and we found the local youth workers appreciative to our training.

It was decided that we would start to work with a mixed group of young people – Protestant and Catholic – and gradually utilise them to recruit participants from both communities. So, there I was sitting in a room with thirty young people, 15 from either side of the community and a handful of local youth workers. The tension was palpable. It really didn't matter if we had the blessing of the leaders or the approval of the youth workers. What mattered was if we could get these young people to mix and look beyond their differences. I introduced myself and explained what the programme was about. Whilst I was clear and focused, I felt the pressure of making this work. Worst case scenario would be a flare up of violence and Sky looking bad, which could lead to them pulling out and …well let's not dwell on what could go wrong.

We did some ice breakers and a few team games, but the two groups remained very much two separate groups. We decided to hold some discussions. Perhaps we could talk this out. Find what they had in common. I was picking topics that I thought were universal such as poverty and cannabis. The conversation was ticking along.

I decided to discuss food and healthy eating. I asked the group if they had given much thought to their consumption. Did they concern themselves with fat content? E numbers? Or eating five portions of fruit and vegetables a day? Throughout my introduction of the subject a young lad named Jake was shaking his head. I stressed the health benefits and the benefits of conscious eating, but Jake's disapproval was constant. In the end I turned to Jake and said:" You seem to have a strong view on this. Would you like to start us off?"

"Well it's all a load of bollocks," said Jake.

I was a bit disappointed but wanted to encourage his contribution." Please say more."

Jake continued." Well I bought a bottle of water which claimed to be from a 10,000 year old spring, but it has a use-by date on the lid."

Perhaps it was because of the tension I had been under, but I thought this was hilarious. I didn't have an answer for it. I couldn't help but burst into laughter and Jake did too. The group hadn't seen this side of my personality. I had tears running down my cheeks. The group started to laugh along with me and Jake. They got the absurdity of what Jake had said and they were laughing along with me. Everyone was laughing so much I just ended the session there and then.

That was a turning point in the course. The group had shared a good laugh together and they started to work together. It led on to one of the best *Reach for the Sky* programmes and it made a lot of long-term cross community relationships.

When I think back to the signing of the Good Friday Agreement one of the outstanding images was of Ian Paisley and Martin McGuinness laughing together. It is worth us all remembering what a powerful human bridge humour can be.

Jo: I'm a person who often reaches for gentle humour to build rapport with people. This does lead to me saying things that I think are humorous sometimes before they have been entirely sense-checked by my brain.

During the King's State Visit to France in 2023, he was enjoying some wonderful Bordeaux gastronomy and was waiting for the local cheese master who had insisted on packaging up some goodies for the King to take away with him. The King was waiting patiently, but it was my job to keep the event to a tight schedule and I needed all of the VIPs to be on stage at this point listening to my ambassador's speech. To try to hurry things along a little, I offered to collect the cheese for His Majesty. A really large wheel of something that looked like Stilton stood imposingly next to us on a table. "Do you want that one as well?" I asked cheekily. "We could roll it to your car."

He looked directly at me and it occurred to me this might have been the type of moment that was quickly regretted in the court of Henry VIII. Charles III however started laughing hard and seemingly taking my confident banter as evidence that I could be trusted to collect a bit of cheese, bounded onto the stage for the speeches. Phew! As the photos were being taken, I was tempted to call out: "Say cheese!" But I felt that maybe that might brie going a bit too far…(**Paul:** Stop it, Jo, I camembert it!)

Why is humour important?

The importance of being in good humour and having inclusive fun can't be overstated. It brings people together; it defuses tension, and it builds bridges.

As humour is a state of mind through which we can see the funny side and appreciating the funny side can help our state of mind. It can form a virtuous circle which will help our mental wellbeing and our physical health.

Keep a track on your state of mind, listen to the people around you. Are they asking you 'what's up' or are they enjoying your company?

Are you spending time with the people who make you laugh? Are you looking for the funny side? Or are you taking life all a bit too seriously?

Perhaps if you change your mind set to a more humorous one, the people around you will change, and the situation will change.

When is it important to be in good humour?

Youth workers often have to deal with sad and serious situations, but no more than doctors, nurses, social workers or police officers.

Lots of people work and live with difficult situations. I got some sound advice from a prison officer when I visited Liverpool's Walton prison. They see some terrible stuff in there. I asked her how she coped. She said, "You know when you deal with such serious issues, you can't be having a bit of fun. A bit of fun is not enough to keep you sane; so you have to have lots and lots of fun."

Humour is a state of mind and fun is an antidote to stress. It is ever present and essential. Therefore, the culture of humour needs to be led from the top. Humour should be encouraged, but it needs to be inclusive and appropriate.

When humour isn't managed properly and the correct tone set, it can go very badly wrong, it can undermine services, damage teams, bring down companies and destroy lives. If you are a leader, don't leave it to chance. Set the tone and be a positive example.

Exercise

Here is an exercise that will help you consider how and when to use humour appropriately in your interactions with others. Note your thoughts as you read the statements. Discuss with others if you can to get another perspective.

Exercise: Humour, Humour! & Humour?

Type of Humour	Is the statement below true?	Consider that...	Your conclusion
Dark	**There is no such thing as bad humour, only the wrong audience.**	Some jokes will miss the mark.	
Self-deprecating	**You've got to laugh at yourself.**	Leaders need respect.	
Physical / slapstick	**Humour must be safe.**	If you throw a thimble of water on someone you have given permission for them to use the fire extinguisher on you.	
Surreal or Absurd	**Life is funny.**	Smiling may help.	
Sarcasm	**Sarcasm is a valid tool.**	Humour is powerful	
Targeted	**Everyone should be the butt of the joke.**	Timing means knowing when to stop.	

Sick	No subject should be off limits.	Humour can aid healing.	
Dry	Humour should be obvious.	Inclusive is best.	

Now answer these 3 questions

Belief – What do you know to be true about humour?

Values – What is important to you about humour in your life?

Action – Are you going to do anything differently?

Conclusion

We can't make you funnier. That's not what this is about, though if you google "jokes for 6-year-olds" you'll find some crackers which can be delivered at random to defuse tension! (**Jo:** My 6-year-old's favourite is - Why did the cow cross the road? He wanted to get to the mooovies.)

Staying in good humour is one of the best weapons you have for your mental and social health. Maintain a light-hearted manner whenever you can and if you do spot something funny, make sure you use it. As long as it is respectful and inclusive, it can build bridges and make life more worth living for everyone.

Paul: Let me share as a final thought on this chapter, one of my favourite stories about humour. On one of the Dali Lama's visits to the UK, he asked to meet people who were working with young people. A number of us were invited to Manchester for a small reception with him. He spoke with wisdom about life and showed curiosity in our work. As the conversation drew to a close, he asked if any of us had a question for him. We all tried to think of a good question. One of the youth workers asked him, "If you could go back in time, what would you say to your teenage self?" Wow! By the nods of heads, I could see that I wasn't the only one thinking that it was a really good question.

"What a silly question!" The Dali Lama said. "Me and another me, talking to me!" He shook his head and laughed. Yes, what a daft question we all thought as we shook our heads in disapproval.

At the end the Dali Lama was being spirited away by his minders and entourage when he made a point of going to the man who had asked the question, took both his hands and made a fuss of him. The man laughed and smiled, and I realised a few things watching them. The Dali Lama had not meant that the question was daft. He meant that the question was funny – it had tickled him.

He must have noticed the man had felt crestfallen due to the misunderstanding and so he went over to connect with the man. The Dali Lama was generous with his time, his wisdom and his sense of humour to ensure the man found the humour of the moment. Thinking back everything the Dali Lama did and said radiated *generosity*, which leads us nicely into our next chapter, since this is also a key attribute of an excellent youth worker.

Attribute 7: Generosity

"We live in a world in which good and evil are exactly equal, and your next act will tip the balance." Jewish proverb

Society is more fragmented than ever. We can shop from home, work from home, have home entertainment systems which even offer each member of the household different content. As we have reduced the need to mix and share space with each other, our sense of community has been eroded. People often act far more harshly with each other in the online world than they ever would in person.

In order to mend our families, our communities, we need to put back the humanity. This is where our next attribute - generosity - comes in. In this chapter we are going to look at generosity from several angles and draw on a number of stories from our lives in the hope that something resonates with you, to help you decide if you are giving and taking in a considered way.

Some people argue that capitalism has gone too far. How can we continue to create billionaires, when we have people still starving in the streets? This widening gap between rich and poor isn't sustainable. We need to learn the lessons of the past. When the struggle becomes too much for ordinary people, society becomes unstable. But if capitalism were reined in and we started giving back more to our communities, to those in need, maybe this clash of classes can be avoided.

Paul: I believe that generosity is a hugely powerful force for good. We are all capable of it. We were once working in one of the poorest areas of Liverpool with a group of 10 unemployed teenage women. The aim of the session was to explore their attitude to money.

These teenagers looked quite intimidating at first. They were abrupt and harsh with each other, and their language would make a docker blush. We decided that before addressing the subject of money we would do some team building. There were several challenges and points were awarded for each task they achieved. This really worked. The group got feedback from the staff after each task, and we were able to highlight how they talked to each other as a weak point. Once the group got 25 points, we moved on to part two.

We turned the 25 points into £25. This was a significant amount of money to these young women, and it was met with a round of applause. There was a catch. We explained that this money was not for them. We wanted them to give this money to a stranger. We were expecting some pushback, but it never came. The group wanted to give the money away. I explained that we could not have all ten of them going out together as that would be terrifying to the poor stranger. The group got together and decided who would go out and to whom they should give the money. The group decided they should give the money to an elderly person.

Three young women went out of the centre with a member of staff, and we awaited their return. When they came back, they told us the story of how they had approached an elderly woman but decided not to speak to her because she had expensive-looking shoes on. They ended up giving the money to a man in his mid-eighties. At first, he wasn't going to take it, but our staff member explained that the young women were taking part in a training programme at the community centre, and he accepted very gratefully, thanking the young women for their generosity and commenting that young people nowadays were so misunderstood.

Back at the centre afterwards, we discussed how it had felt to do this. Was it generous to give something away that you don't need? Can you be kind without money? How many different ways were there to be kind and generous? Who were the kindest people they knew?

We were about to move on when there was a knock on the door. It was the elderly man. He handed in some flowers and a thank you card. The man had been completely blown away by their kindness. He explained that he now lived alone and said he wished his wife was still alive so he could tell her this story. There wasn't a dry eye in the house, and we had a really meaningful conversation about what it means to be kind and generous.

I've always found that young people love to have the opportunity to be generous. Here is another example which is from my work at Vibe.

We were holding a Halloween party at one of our community centres. I was working in my office when one of my colleagues knocked at the door. It was time to judge the fancy dress competition, and they wanted me to do it. I walked out to see over a hundred little vampires, Frankenstein's monsters, witches etc. The prize was a food hamper which the local shops had donated. It had everything in it from tins of beans to chocolate and cheese.

The children were calling and shouting as I walked amongst them. Some of the costumes were amazing and wouldn't have been out of place on a Hollywood movie set. I noticed one young girl who was 8 or 9 years old. She was standing quietly, her outfit obviously homemade. Just a white powdered face some ragged clothes and a mascara painted scar. I wasn't sure what the criteria for the winner was, but I picked her because my heart went out to her. She was really surprised and totally overjoyed.

It turns out that she was one of the *Me Time* children. These are children who come from struggling families and would not have been able to attend without extra support. Vibe staff had picked them up in a minibus and had dressed them up en route. I honestly didn't know, but I totally picked the right child to win. The Vibe staff fed back to me that as they drove the children home in the minibus, the young girl shared the hamper out with the other children.

From my experience young people can be very generous, they just need the opportunity. Given the opportunity, it can stick with them for a lifetime.

The camel and the needle

A staff member at the Vibe charity recently passed me the contact email of a billionaire who was a friend of a friend. He suggested I contacted them for a charitable donation. I crafted what I thought was a persuasive email, but soon got a curt reply saying they were "fully extended" at this time. This made me pause and consider, somewhat perplexed: What does it mean to be fully extended when you own a vast business empire and people are desperate for support? I was very disappointed. I said to a friend of mine that I couldn't be a person who had thousands of millions of pounds and not be more willing to help people. He replied, "And that is why you will never be a billionaire." I concluded to myself that real generosity is to give something you would like to keep, not giving away things (including money) that you don't need.

I was left with a question which I now pose to you: Would you rather have your current money and be generous or rich and selfish?

Let me tell you about one of my mentors, an amazing woman named Liz Cross. Liz has helped me out of many a sticky situation by helping me to be more generous. We would chat over lunch, and I would often share a story of an annoying or egotistical person wanting Liz to agree with me, but she would ask me questions like: What gift can you offer this person to help them understand? If you forgive them, will you both feel better? Please don't misunderstand. Liz is no push over. She is about 5'2" but she is a totally formidable and fearless powerhouse. She has just thankfully decided to live a life that puts good into the world.

One day Liz was walking from one meeting to another through Manchester when a man stood in front of her brandishing a knife and demanding her money. Liz looked the man in the eye and said, "I will give you money but first, you must tell me what has brought you to this position in your life." The man was totally shocked and welled up. "Come on," Liz said. "Let me take you for a coffee." The man agreed and got an hour of Liz's time, which is worth so much more than the cash she also decided to give him.

Liz is so much more advanced than me in this way of being. I have learned so much from her, but I have so much more to learn.

The gift of advice

Another person I have learned from in this area is the double gold medallist Olympian Dame Kelly Holmes. Some years ago, Kelly noticed that too many athletes struggle once they retire. She knew that these athletes have exceptional drive, determination and focus. Kelly was also concerned that far too many young people were struggling in society due to a lack of direction, purpose, and confidence. So, Kelly decided to start a charity to bring athletes and young people together and the amazing

Dame Kelly Holmes Trust was born. I was an advisor to No.10 Downing Street at the time and I met Kelly when she came in to meet the then Prime Minister David Cameron.

I was very impressed by Kelly. Let's face it, she could have retired and put her feet up, but she was determined to help people, generously giving of her time and energy. I was also impressed that she was very honest about what was working and what wasn't going so well in her work.

Kelly shared with me that whilst the athletes had the attributes the young people needed, the athletes and young people were struggling to relate to each other. Top athletes aren't youth workers. They were used to working with sports coaches who have a more direct, no-nonsense, results-focused approach. Many of the young people were rebelling against this methodology.

Kelly turned to me and asked if I could help her.

When you meet someone as charismatic and generous as Kelly it is virtually impossible to turn her down. Besides, I was delighted that she recognised the expertise of youth workers. This is to the heart of what this book is about. These athletes were already amazing people and training them in youth works skills, techniques and activities made them an awesome team. They were an absolute pleasure to train, and that charity now delivers incredible results.

Group photos were the only downside of this work for me. It's not easy being photographed next to 40 athletes! They were lovely though and very appreciative of our support. It seemed to me that showing appreciation is another form of generosity.

I can't leave this section without sharing one of my claims to fame. Having worked with Kelly and her team for some years, she knew I had run 10 marathons. (I must have let it slip out in one or seven of our conversations.) When Kelly put her name down to run her first ever marathon, the London Marathon, she asked me if I had any tips. I thought for a moment and gave her the following advice.

All marathon runners are afraid of *The Wall*. For those readers who aren't marathon runners let me explain. *The Wall* hits around the 20-mile mark. You have burnt up all the reserves in your legs and you still have six miles left to run. It is agony and like running into a wall, you really struggle to move forward. It is common to see people starting walking or giving up entirely.

It happened to me several times and then on one New York Marathon run, I was approaching the 20-mile mark with the usual trepidation when a woman was standing at the side of the road holding up a placard with 4 words on: "THERE IS NO WALL." The woman shouted it at me, "There is no wall!"

I repeated it to myself. "There is no wall." The fear melted away and I got a surge of energy. I was so grateful to that woman. I have no idea who she was but to make a placard and stand at the 20-mile mark, just to help people who were struggling was a very kind and generous thing to do.

I gave Kelly my tip. "There is no wall."

I was at an event a few weeks after Kelly had successfully completed the London Marathon. I was in the audience and Kelly was speaking on the stage. She noticed me and shouted, "There is no wall!" with the biggest grin on her face.

So, one of my claims to fame is that I helped Dame Kelly Holmes get a medal. (Ok not one of her Olympic medals but hey.)

I wonder how many walls only exist in our minds. Perhaps one of the most kind and generous things we can do is to help people to help themselves and let go of false limitations.

What could you the reader achieve if you started with the belief that ......*there is no wall.*

Little things make a lifetime of difference

Jo: This concept of generosity is important to me. As someone who has been a civil servant for over 20 years, I have a fundamental belief in being generous with your time to help others. This is where we really move from helping ourselves to helping others and helping our communities.

I believe that generosity is like karma. What you give, you will receive back in other ways. This goes for businesses and employers too. There are many studies that show that people work harder if organisations are generous with their benefits, going beyond what they must legally provide.

Generosity is a broad concept. One aspect which is very powerful as a senior leader is being generous with your time, since others know and appreciate how precious it is.

I was once in Sweden on a training camp to learn skills for freefall formation skydiving. (Holding hands to make pretty patterns in the sky whilst plummeting at 120mph. I appreciate, not everyone's idea of fun.) On one jump, as I deployed my parachute, nothing happened. I quickly detached from the main parachute and released the reserve, which thankfully opened perfectly, albeit only a few seconds before impact. I only just had time to pull the brakes before I hit a farmer's field with thankfully only a gentle bump.

It was genuinely a moment when I thought I was about to die. Travelling 120mph getting very close to the ground with a malfunctioning parachute, my brain had informed me that I was going to die. Thankfully not, but I was properly shaken. I had also, in detaching from the main parachute, lost this very expensive piece of kit in the overgrown cornfield. After a large cup of sweet tea to help manage the shock, I set out to scour the field for my parachute.

"Hang on," came a shout. "I'll help you look." I was amazed. Kate Cooper-Jensen - skydiving superstar and organiser of the whole event - was giving up her very precious time to help me trudge through a field? "I'll come too," offered Joe Bickerton, someone who I'd judged up until that point as being a bit of a scary, tough military-type. (I have since got to know Joe much better as he married one of my close friends who will find it hilarious that I ever thought him to be scary.)

I remember their generosity to this day, 15 years later. At that time, I was still a pretty junior skydiver, and they were much more experienced than me. They weren't close friends, but they generously gave up their time to help me, when they could have been doing a thousand things more fun than searching (in vain as it turned out) for my lost parachute (a combined harvester would sadly find it first some weeks later). I hugely appreciated their support and company, especially at a time when I was feeling quite wobbly. For the rest of my skydiving career, when someone lost a piece of kit in a field (not an entirely uncommon occurrence), I was the first to offer to help look for it.

As a busy manager or senior leader, you often find it difficult to be generous with your time though, for obvious practical reasons. To this I suggest, being generous with your attention instead.

In my first overseas posting, as a UK negotiator in Brussels, I worked for an incredibly effective and impressive lady called Shan Morgan. To give you an idea of just how impressive, Shan would go on to be our Deputy Ambassador to the European Union and then the most senior civil servant in the Welsh Government. She was high-performing and driven and certainly didn't have any "spare time". She had a great system though. When she was busy, her door was closed. When it was open, you could drop in and speak to her. That's when the magic would happen. If you asked to speak to her, she would give you her absolute focus, her entire attention. She would listen attentively, asking questions, supporting you to come up with your own ideas for solutions and offering guidance. She didn't have lots of time to spare, but the time she gave you was such high quality, it was transformative. As well as very helpful in many practical ways, it was massively motivating for a young civil servant like me to have such rich input from someone so talented and experienced.

She gave generously and inspired me to always try to do the same. When I became a manager myself, I had a post-it on the side of my computer saying "BE HERE NOW", meaning: focus on the person who is in front of you. If you are not giving your attention to a member of your team when they come speak to you, it can be massively demotivating as well as a waste of everyone's precious time. Be generous to those you manage. Give them your attention, even when time in scarce, and it will pay dividends.

People are a package

I once got injured skydiving and felt terribly guilty about not being as efficient at work because of this. "You must be so frustrated with me," I said to my boss at the time, a lady called Jackie Harrop. "You must think it's ridiculous that I've gone off skydiving and now can't get into the office I have hurt my leg." She smiled. "People are a package," she smiled reassuringly. She explained that during a career or even during a particular job, there will be times when someone is performing well and other times that they have other things going on: a divorce, an illness, a bad leg. She was generous and kind in my time of vulnerability and that was incredibly motivating for me to work even harder for her when I got back to work. I often use the same words with my own teams now, when someone is feeling bad that they can't give their all. Our best teachers and mentors generously give us gifts that keep on giving.

The Kindness of Strangers

Paul: The generosity of strangers can have a massive impact on us too.

It was never my intention to become a youth worker. When I left school, I wanted to join the Special Air Service (SAS). That seemed like an adventurous *go get 'em* lifestyle. I knew that not many people made it into the SAS, so I set about formulating a plan. Over the next four years I became a black belt in karate, I became an electrician, and I joined the territorial army parachute regiment. The idea being, that all these things would improve my chances of getting into the SAS and if I was unsuccessful, they would give me something to fall back on. Eventually an opportunity came up to attend a survival course in Germany run by the SAS, so I jumped at it.

The training wasn't just about survival. It also included escaping and evading the enemy plus resistance to interrogation. I can't go into too much detail, but I can say that I quickly realised that I didn't want to join them. My tendency to question everything didn't make us a good fit.

The course was fascinating though. It built up to a final challenge where we would have to make our way across Germany while being hunted down. I spent 72 hours wet and tired, travelled at night and sleeping rough during the day. In the early morning of day four I had had enough of this stupid exercise. I was drenched wet through, knackered and hungry. I was lost somewhere in Germany, and I didn't want to join the SAS anyway.

I walked up to a farmhouse and knocked on the door. A German woman in her thirties with two young children answered. I handed her the card in German that we had been given which explained that I was on a training exercise. She looked me up and down and gestured me in. This was quite a poor looking family. There were some clothes drying in front of a real fire. She moved the clothes and beckoned me forwards to get a warm. I sat by the fire and before long I noticed the steam coming off my clothes.

A man - the farmer - came home and the couple had a conversation in concerned tones. She showed him the card. They called me to the table, and we sat and ate a meal together. It was chicken, cabbage, and potatoes. It was the nicest meal I have ever had in my life, before or since. I got my mojo back. I used basic English and sign language to ask them how to find my destination. They pointed me in the right direction, I thanked them and remembering to retrieve the card, I left.

I had a spring in my step and a couple of hours later I managed to reach the target village. Unfortunately for me, this wasn't the end of the gruelling training, as the team had a few more nasty surprises in store for us. But I had a full belly thanks to the kindness of strangers. In the tougher moments, I would give a little smile to myself and think 'you will never know.' The kindness of those strangers had gone a long way.

Whilst it turned out that joining the SAS wasn't the right goal for me, I also realised that by having a goal, I was moving forward and learning many things that helped to shape my future direction.

I bring learning to my youth work practice from everything I have done in my life. Being an electrician, I learned how my work reflects on me, from karate I learned humility and from the paras I learned teamwork. But if I had to hold on to one important lesson from my SAS journey, it is to be kind and generous to strangers - a lesson I learned from a German family who I don't know and will never meet again but to whom I will be eternally grateful for the nicest meal I ever had.

Due to such experiences, I have a great deal of faith in humanity. If most people were selfish, society couldn't function. But I fundamentally believe that most people are kind. That's why we have charities, first aiders, blood donors and volunteers. People rightfully look after themselves, but many people also care for others.

Being generous to yourself

In fact, some people can be far more generous, forgiving and kind to other people than they are to themselves. They are often more critical and profoundly negative when thinking about themselves. If this is you, give yourself a break! You wouldn't talk like that to anyone else, so why not focus on your qualities and achievements rather than giving yourself a hard time.

Some people cannot see their glass as half-full as they are too focused on seeing the empty half. Our brain does this to protect us: we need to be aware of problems in order to overcome them. This was particularly important when our problems were: we have no food, we need to go kill a woolly mammoth. But most of us don't need our survival instincts to be that well-honed anymore. Our basic needs are mostly met with greater ease than our neanderthal ancestors. We now need to tackle the instinctive negativity we find popping into our mind, or it can manifest itself as imposter syndrome or a sense of never feeling good enough.

There are two main reasons our mind focuses on our problems, shortcomings and failures:

1. To avoid them in future
2. To frighten ourselves into accomplishing our goals

But this is unhelpful and negative thinking when it becomes too dominant and will drain your energy.

To avoid focusing on our shortcomings, we must deliberately focus on our qualities and successes. This is not about being boastful. It is about focusing on the positives and giving yourself a pat on the back (at least for trying). Being overly self-critical is damaging to our mental health and our resilience.

It is also unhealthy to be driven by fear but is far more common that you may think. Imagine you want to run across a field in under a minute. Are you more likely to achieve this if there is a pot of gold at the finishing line or if there is a tiger chasing you? Most people would be more motivated by getting away from a tiger. But if they achieve the goal, they don't get a sense of accomplishment, they get a sense of relief. You can never satisfy the tiger in your mind because it is not real. I have helped many people to realise this, but some like to keep it anyway (it is their way of succeeding) and go through their lives never getting a true sense of achievement.

It's all in your mind, so have a kind mind. Be generous with yourself and motivate yourself with a vision of success that you can celebrate when you achieve, not with a fear of failure that can never be satisfied.

Jo: Being generous towards yourself is also a lesson I have had to learn the hard way. As someone very focused on high achievement, I've sometimes pushed myself too hard leading to times of stress, burn-out and illness.

I used to be on the British Skydiving squad, representing my country at formation skydiving. One training camp, I had a real breakthrough in my mindset. I had an awful cold and was struggling to keep up with the punishing training regime. Landing from a jump where I had struggled for concentration, I got completely frustrated with myself and was in tears that I hadn't performed up to standard. Our coach – an inspirational and very talented Italian skydiver Marco Arrigo - came over to me, having watched the video of the jump. He asked me why I was getting so frustrated. The jump was perfectly fine. And anyway, it was only a training jump. I explained that I knew I could do better but felt like I was letting the team down and myself by being under the weather. "You can't always be at 100%," he said. "And you at 60% is better than most people at 100%."

In the years since, I've used this with other people who are beating themselves up unnecessarily - and frequently had to remind myself too. When I was a new mum and struggling with a sleepless nights after I'd gone back to work, I'd remind myself that I was the very best person to be doing my job (and the very best mum for my child) and that if I wasn't firing on all cylinders for a little while, that was still pretty damn good! I offer this advice parents in the office, when they feel guilty about having to get home for the kids, whilst our younger colleagues can pull a few extra hours and work into the evening. Maybe the youngsters can put in extra hours, but those who are parents bring different experiences. We all have our strengths. We need to remember that and use it to reassure ourselves when we are feeling unsure.

Conclusion

We are sure that by now you have realised that this is not an instructional book which is going to tell you how to live your life. We offer guidance

162

and an opportunity for reflection. It is very much for you to decide if you want to be generous with your time, money, advice, help and support.

There is a school of thought that states that it's a dog-eat-dog world and you should 'look after number one.' Our take on that is that you will not learn anything worth knowing at that school! If you really want to get the most out of life, apply the youth worker school of generous thinking and reap the benefits that this sows for yourself and others.

We are not saying that you must always put yourself second, but if you are prepared to see if the world is a better place with more generosity, challenge yourself to an act of generosity tomorrow and see what happens!

Generosity is a type of kindness – and youth workers are certainly kind-hearted souls - but we wouldn't want you to think that youth workers are a push over. Far from it and sometimes they certainly have to deal out some tough love. This takes us to our next attribute: *kindness with strength*.

Attribute 8: Kindness with Strength

Great youth workers are compassionate and kind. They have to build bridges, make connections and gain trust. They challenge their clients to help them change and grow. But don't mistake this kindness for letting young people get away with anything. Great youth workers also have to be strong and enforce boundaries. They need to be consistent and take difficult decisions. We are not going to lie to you: this is a difficult balance to strike.

Great youth workers are excellent at judging this. If on day one of a new course there's a lot of swearing and messing around from the young people, you need to take time to build a relationship to be able to address these behaviours. Laying down the law for minor transgressions on day one will get you exactly nowhere. But you also need to know when enough is enough.

As parents, with the responsibility of bringing up the next generation, it is also crucial to get this right. Be too soft and we spoil our children. Be too tough and we risk alienating them and damaging them emotionally.

Paul: A youth worker once told me about a teenage girl she was working with who was known to be a prolific shoplifter. The youth worker spoke to the girl's father and warned him that he needed to get control of the situation as the young woman would inevitably be caught. The father reassured the youth worker that he was taking this really seriously and he would stop the girl stealing…right after his birthday! I can't really vouch for this story being 100% true! But the message is still important. Sometimes we avoid challenging others as we feel that it is just too difficult, embarrassing or awkward. It is surprising what we can justify to ourselves.

As leaders and managers, we may be friendly with our teams, but we must be able to set expectations and challenge behaviour or lose respect. As managers too of what is known as Generation Z – young people born between the late 1990s and early 2010s. Those Gen Z-ers in the workplace ask for more compassion and understanding of their personal needs (a contrast with earlier generations) but a job still needs to get done.

Getting this balance of kindness with strength, including compassionate challenge is important for all of us to have healthy families, workplaces and communities.

Compassionate Challenge

Challenging their young clients is a key part of the youth worker role. It is how we support them to grow and develop. To move beyond their difficulties. To help them develop critical thinking. To support young people to develop their own ideas around integrity. A lot of people don't want to examine their beliefs, values and actions. It's uncomfortable. Particularly teenagers who think they know best or have had their trust in adults damaged. But these young people really benefit from this challenge. It is not a kindness to leave them as they are.

The way youth workers go about this challenge is however crucial. Great youth workers challenge with compassion based on trust, built through engagement. They challenge not to persuade their clients to change their way of thinking, but to help them on their journey. Youth workers structure interventions around physical, mental and social challenges. Physical challenges might be outdoor pursuits like abseiling and rock climbing. Mental challenges include budget management, problem solving exercises. Social challenges could be team working activities or public speaking. By providing such activities, this also leads to emotional challenges as young people are pushed out of - and then expand - their comfort zone.

Paul: Several years ago, a brilliant youth worker I know called Tony Smith ran a programme in a Young Offender Institute in Preston for 15 young people who were serving time for anti-social behaviour. Development of ethics is important to healthy relationships, so some of Tony's interventions with the group focused on putting a moral dilemma to them.

In one exercise Tony offered each of them 50p if they would badmouth their own football team. A few passionate supporters refused, so they were out of the game. He then asked who in the remaining group was prepared to insult him to his face for £1. Again, a few were uncomfortable that this crossed a line for them, and they dropped out.

Tony then asked:" Who would sign a petition for all pandas to be killed for £2?" The stakes were getting higher! Finally, we got down to the final five. Tony put a toddler's toy train in the middle of the floor and explained that this was a toy he would send to a child who was growing up in a children's home or he would give £3 to anyone who would smash it up. Now this caused most of them to refuse. Several of them had grown up in the care system with few toys. Left was just one tough guy. He raised his foot above the toy train. Everyone in the room held their breath. He brought down his foot again and again smashing it. The whole room was shocked. He had crossed a line.

"How do you feel?" Tony asked as he handed him the three quid. He hung his head. "I thought it would impress everyone, but it didn't. I guess that's why I'm in here." It was a breakthrough moment achieved by pushing the group well out of their comfort zone.

So how might we put this attribute into action in other contexts?

I was once travelling with a group of youth workers and one - Dan - was getting irate about not being allowed to take an extra bag on the plane. He was fuming and shouting at the check-in staff. As he came to sit back down, complaining loudly to anyone in earshot, our colleague Sue leaned over to him, put a gentle hand on his arm and quietly asked, "Is this how you want to be?"

He stopped for a moment, stood up and got back in the queue for the counter. The guy on the check-in desk looked up with wary eyes. "I'm sorry," said Dan. "I just came over to apologise. I was very rude, and it was uncalled for. I'm sorry." The guy looked back at him. "Let's see what we can do about your extra bag," he smiled. Sue's compassionate challenge had turned everyone's day around.

Jo: For me as someone who manages and coaches others, this is all about enabling personal and professional growth. It might feel like kindness not to challenge people too much, but it's outside of the comfort zone where change can happen.

As a manager, it is important to get the balance right. If you throw someone in at the deep end and they really can't swim, you are neglecting your duty of care to them as well as your responsibility to deliver for your organisation. But by stretching people to do things that they think they can't, providing just enough support, this can transform people as workers, but also in their attitudes towards themselves. This goes for parenting too.

This requires a coaching mindset. When someone comes to you for an answer, wanting to be provided with the solution to a problem, ask yourself if this is a coachable moment. Have a few open questions ready: "What would you suggest as the way forward?" "What other experiences can we draw on to help us think about this?"

When we moved to China as a family, I thought it was a kindness to pick up lots of basic tasks from my husband who can't speak Chinese. Whenever we move to a new country, it's a huge amount of energy to establish new networks and friendship groups, figure out the local neighbourhood, set up new routines. When we moved to China, these challenges were even more complicated by a difficult foreign language being part of the mix.

At the beginning of our posting, even leaving the compound where we lived was complicated, since it involved negotiating with Chinese taxi drivers to take us into town which was some miles away. In theory, with the taxi app we used, there was no need to talk to a driver. They had all the information in the app to get you from A to B. But some of them really seemed to like to talk. No sooner had you booked your ride in the app, they were calling you to discuss your journey. Although my level of Chinese was pretty decent, it was often difficult to decipher what they were calling about, so I would just repeat my journey details back to them and they'd come pick us up.

To start with, I just dealt with the bookings myself as my husband found it understandably more stressful, but it soon became clear that he was rarely leaving the compound where we lived if I wasn't with him. I gradually started to get him to book the cab when we were going out together, giving him advice on what to do if they called (ignore it and send a short message which they could translate in the app). To begin with, he was still reluctant to do it if I wasn't there, but practice made perfect and whilst I don't think he ever got comfortable with it, he made it work and it opened up the city to him. I realised that my earlier kindness hadn't been really what he needed. He had needed to overcome the challenge himself in order to thrive in the new environment.

Try this exercise to analyse and develop your compassionate challenge skills:

Exercise: The Map of Compassionate Challenge (20 minutes)

In everyday life, we often need to challenge others, but don't always know how best to go about it. So how can we be better at challenging? Sometimes it is normal to be unhappy with something but taking that emotion into the challenge can be counterproductive. Sometimes we need to take control of a situation. We need to keep in mind thought that when we are angry and controlling however, we risk our challenge not succeeding and we are certainly not developing people.

The diagram on the next page is designed to help you to consider your approach to someone you want to coach to make a change and notice how often you are being developmental and how often you are being controlling.

	Questioning		
Angry	(Passive) Aggressive	**Compassionate** **Challenge**	**Caring**
	Bullying	Instructing	
	Controlling		

Consider the four areas above:

1. Angry questioning = (Passive) aggressive
2. Caring questions = Compassionate challenge
3. Angry controlling = Bullying
4. Caring controlling = Instruction

Questions:

Give examples of when you know you have been in each section.

As a percentage how much time do you spend in each area?

Are there some people who you tend to take you to a particular area? Why is that?

Is there anything you would like to change?

Tough Love

As mentioned, we should not mistake this compassion for being soft or going easy on others. Great youth workers demonstrate this <u>kindness alongside strength</u>. Because sometimes a bit of tough love is needed.

Paul: Let me give you an example. I had once organised a residential outward-bound course for a group of 20 young people. Now these types of interventions take a lot of organising. A huge amount of effort had gone in from me and my team. Part of it was to prepare the young people and make sure they were in a good frame of mind to make the most of the experience. As part of our preparations, we discussed ground rules with the young people. We were worried that they might smoke cannabis, so agreed with them that no drugs were allowed, or they'd be sent home. Agreeing to this was a criterion for coming on the residential and all the young people signed up to the pledge.

Then on the first night, we smelt it. The unmistakable aroma of our agreement being broken! I called them all together and asked them to own up. Five of the group sheepishly did.

I discussed it with my team. What message did we want to send? If we allowed them to break the agreement and get away with it, they would continue to break the rules. It might lead others to break the rules too and our work would be a real uphill battle. It felt harsh, but we stuck to our guns and sent the young people home. The impact on those left on the course was dramatic. They took it really seriously, engaged with us and got huge amounts out of the week. They others were gutted - and we were gutted for them - and went home but were allowed to apply for future residential when they were ready to abide by the rules. A bit of tough love was needed to get a good outcome for the group.

Try this exercise to consider whether you are getting this balance right in your relationships.

Exercise: Kind and Strong (20 minutes)

This exercise will help you to notice if you are off target with your behaviour towards other people and help you to become more purposeful and impactful.

The model below maps out kindness and strength so that you can plot where your behaviour fits on the graph.

Kind + strong = Assertive	**Strong**	Strong but unkind = Bully
Kind		**Unkind**
Kind but weak = Push over	**Weak**	Weak and unkind = Reactive

Note down your answers:

1. Can you think of an example of your behaviour for each quadrant?

  1. In which quadrant do you spend most of your time?

  2. Are there particular people in your life you struggle to find the balance with?

  3. When do you find it hard to strike the right balance?

  4. What support can you get, or actions can you take to stay in the assertive (top left) quadrant?

Jo: So how might we put this attribute into action in a parenting context? As a parent, this resonates most with me in my dealings with my 6-year-old. What is best for someone and what seems like kindness, are often very different things when put through the judgement of a small child! A simple example. Recently my son came home from school desperate (he said) for chocolate. I gave him the leftover piece of his chocolaty birthday cake. It ruined his dinner, and he bounced off the walls until finally the sugar crash wore off and he passed out at bedtime.

So why did I give it to him when I knew it was a bad idea? Maybe I was trying to be liked. He often tells me he likes Daddy more as he gives him more treats. I was also trying to stop him nagging me, as I needed to complete some work. I was also feeling guilty about having to travel for work that week. On reflection, all these things were about my needs, not about doing what was the best for him. The dreadful evening that resulted was certainly a kindness to neither of us. Saying no would have been a better outcome: kind and strong.

In a professional context too, we often have to disappoint people in order to deliver our goals e.g. not letting someone take the day off when there's a big deadline looming. But approaching difficult conversations with care and compassion will always make them more successful. There are certainly more kind and less kind ways for delivering a message that is tough for people to hear.

For example, I once oversaw a large restructuring of Harrow Council's Children's Services. The Director of Children's Services Catherine Doran had recently arrived to find that the department's budget had been dramatically cut and she could see that their systems and structures needed updating. Catherine knew that it was going to be tough on the staff involved, but significant restructuring was vital to make sure that the children and young people of Harrow got the services they needed.

Throughout, Catherine's approach was to be compassionate with individuals without losing our clear focus on delivery. She asked those of us working on the project to consider: How could we carry out the process most efficiently so as to not drag out for some what would inevitably be a painful experience? What support did people need through this process? For those who would be made redundant, how could we help prepare them for applying for new jobs?

Despite this being the biggest restructuring in the Council's history, including a number of redundancies and hundreds of people being moved into different roles in new locations, the process went smoothly. I think this is because we listened to people and showed we really did care about them by supporting them every way we reasonably could.

Over the course of the last 25 years at work, I've had to let people go on several occasions. It's never easy, but it is sometimes an act of kindness to the individual that they don't continue in a job for which they are unsuited. Certainly, it is often an act of kindness to the health of the organisation and the wider team to move someone on who is in a bad place. Supporting them to find something for which they are a better fit can be a kindness.

This also goes for managing poor performance of a member of staff. It might seem kinder to allow them to carry on without challenging their lack of delivery or poor behaviour. But this is rarely kind for the wider team or good for the health of the organisation. We all need to abide by clear boundaries, rules and expectations to have healthy organisations. When these codes are transgressed, managers and leaders need to challenge and with compassion, improvements can be made, leading to greater job satisfaction of the individual and a more productive, happier team. Kind but strong. Strong but kind.

Conclusion

You can see that great youth workers don't just play Mr-Nice-Guy to get young people on side. Whilst they build rapport and connection with young people, their job is to challenge young people and when things go too far, teach them that there are boundaries that must be respected. Sometimes some tough love is required for individuals and organisations to be healthy and for us to be fair to all as managers and leaders. Certainly, as parents, we need to balance kindness and doing the right thing, which doesn't always make us popular with our kids!

By building the right relationship, people will know you care for them, but that you will also make a stand when needed. It is through this consistency that they build respect for you. They trust you and they believe in you. Even whilst being "tough", whilst insisting on boundaries and managing expectations, if it comes from a place of kindness and compassion, action is likely to be more successful.

It's clear that challenging - compassionately - is a key way to nurture growth in others. This expands our impact beyond ourselves, which is as important to managers, leaders, partners and parents as it is to youth workers. *The ability to release untapped potential* is a very powerful youth worker attribute, so let's explore it in more detail in the next chapter.

Attribute 9: The Ability to Unlock Potential

There is a Cherokee Indian legend about the battle between the good and the bad within us. A grandfather is teaching his grandson about life and explains that each of us has two wolves inside us, locked in battle. One wolf is evil - angry, vicious, arrogant, consumed by lies, false pride and ego. The other is good - all joy, peace, love, humility, kindness, truth and compassion. "Which wolf will win?" Asks the boy. The old man replies, "The one that you feed."

In earlier chapters, we have explored how to do more to unlock your own potential. We'll now concentrate on how to see and unlock the potential in others.

Great youth workers see the potential for good in their clients, no matter how challenging their behaviour. They understand that people can be more tomorrow than they are today. They help young people see this in themselves. Teenagers who have gone off the rails, have often been written off by those around them, so is it any wonder they can't see the potential within themselves to take a different course?

Great youth workers can turn things around for young people where everyone else has given up on them: their family, other professionals, the system. They can inspire these young people away from gangs, away from suicidal thoughts, away from making bad decisions.

Maybe you too have lost your way recently and aren't reaching your full potential. In the western world, many cultures are facing a crisis of confidence. A 2019 survey (by Yakult UK) found that 80% of Brits said that their lives lack purpose. This figure rises to 89% for young people. Over a third of people wish that they could start their lives over again. Anxiety and depression are on the rise throughout the developed world. By focusing on unlocking potential, you can help yourself and others succeed and find happiness.

If you could help some of those 80% of the people around you - and yourself - to feel more purpose in their lives, imagine what a positive impact you would have on the world.

Paul: I once worked with a lad Michael who was seemingly unremarkable in his group. Michael wasn't loud, wasn't particularly difficult, but was also disengaged. He was one of those who could have easily got in with the wrong crowd and this would have been a very different story.

One day, I took the group rock climbing, as part of a physical challenge - often used by youth workers to get young people out of their comfort zone. Michael just adored it. He came alight. He came to me afterwards and asked if we could go again. That wasn't at all the plan, but I could see the fire in his eyes and so I arranged for him to go again. And again. It was the making of him. He really got into the sport and started working in a climbing store. (Helpfully getting me a 20% discount!)

Michael now climbs all over the world, teaching others, leading them on complicated ice climbs. It's not just his own life which was transformed. He touches the lives of others incredibly positively. If I had just said "no we are doing a different activity next week" his life may have been completely different.

"Don't try to rush progress. Remember -- a step forward, no matter how small, is a step in the right direction. Keep believing." Kara Goucher

I was once working in Leicester with an amazing youth worker called Sianette Owen (one of those youth workers worth their weight in gold) - known to everyone as Shin - to support young people from troubled families. This was an amazing piece of work. Top notch, because the forward-thinking council asked us to work separately with children and their parents and then bring them together for a final team building challenge.

I am not sure what you, the reader, conjure up in your minds when I say 'troubled families' but these people and their children were lovely. They were struggling, often for no reason of their own. Perhaps through the sudden loss of a loved one, an illness or redundancy. Sometimes all three. These families were not off the rails. They were doing their very best with the hand they had been dealt and it was a privilege to support them. Our role was to help their relationships and to rebuild their confidence.

Shin and I were working with a group of eight children who were around 10 years old. They were quite immature compared to some of the streetwise 10-year-olds we were used to working with in London, Newcastle or Manchester. Some of them brought toys in with them and one lad (who we will call Bobby) was a selective mute. I hadn't worked with selective mutism before. It is an anxiety disorder. The term refers to someone who is able to speak but does not. The reason in this child's case was that he had found his mother's body after she had died (of natural causes).

We got to work with them one evening a week for five weeks. It was hard work. Not because they were challenging our authority, but because they would crumple under any challenge or question. There would be tears and tantrums from the group, but never from Bobby who was very supportive in his own way. He would put his arm around tearful group members or bring them their toy.

The plan was to work them up to a children's challenge and then they would face a harder challenge with their parents. We didn't want a challenge that was too easy as we needed an activity that would engender a sense of achievement.

As all the children liked computer games, we used that format to set them a real-life challenge. The group had eight tasks to complete. The tasks were like those you would see at a fairground. Using hoops, balls, hooks and darts. Fun but with a catch. Each task had to be successfully completed sequentially. Meaning if one task is failed the group would need (like in a computer game) to start again.

Like climbing a ladder, the group would get so far up only to fall back down to the start. Time after time they failed. The furthest the group of children got was to task number eight when they failed and returned to number one. But they never quit. They showed tremendous determination, and we could not have been prouder of them and although they had not completed the challenge, they were proud of their efforts. Interestingly the parents took a similar task the following day and also failed. The following week the final challenge took place - a combined challenge for the parents and children to join forces.

The combined group made several attempts and managed to get to task number ten, in which one of the children needed to throw a ball into a bucket for the whole team to win. There was no time to make a further attempt, so this one throw was win or lose.

I handed the ball to Bobby.

I was a little terrified. It would be amazing if he scored, but what if he missed? Although Bobby never spoke, I knew he was tough. I knew he would handle it. Bobby threw the ball and there was total silence.

The ball hit the rim and fell back into the bucket. There was a huge cheer, and the parents and children celebrated like they had won the world cup. Hugs, dancing and singing.

When things settled down, we sat in a circle and people spoke of their pride and their love for one another. I congratulated the families and said how much of a privilege it had been to work with them and that this brought the programme to a close. "Hang on," said Shin." Would you like to say something, Bobby?"

Bobby nodded and having not spoken a word for over five years, he said in a calm, but strong voice:" Thanks, everyone." There wasn't a dry eye in the house.

The power that can be unleashed when you see and nurture the potential in others applies to people at all stages in their life, not just young people. A few years ago, Cumbria got some money to try innovative approaches to getting those considered "unemployable" back into the workforce and reached out to me and my team. Shin had taken the first cohort, and I was doing the second. To me it was quickly clear that the main barrier to work for the poor souls sent on this mandatory training ("or they'll cut our dole") was that they themselves believed that they were unemployable. None of them actually thought that they could secure a job.

I had just started the course on day one when a fist banged against the window. A woman was jumping up and down outside the training room trying to get our attention. I opened the window. She shouted past me to the group. "I did this course last week with Sianette! It's a brilliant course! I've just got a job!"

Her energy and her story lifted the room. They started to believe. The lady - Claire - had stopped believing in herself, but Shin had believed in her and worked with her on her relationship with herself. And here Claire was, glowing and excited about the opportunity ahead of her. Claire was the very best advert for what we were trying to do. Those on the course realised that maybe they weren't unemployable after all! Maybe it was worth giving it a try. Maybe, like Claire, this could be the turning point. It made my job that week a great deal easier.

How often have you dismissed someone as a lost cause or a waste of your time? In fact, potential can be residing in some of the least obvious places.

Dragons Den star Deborah Meaden tells a story about the time that someone came into the den and got his numbers so wrong (out by a multiple of 1000!) that she quickly announced herself out, shaking her head in disbelief. But two of the other dragons - Peter Jones and Richard Farley - had seen something else. They had not seen a man poor at maths (and anyway they had plenty of accountants who could crunch the numbers). They had seen charm, charisma and an engaging product. According to the Sunday Times Rich List, Levi Roots is now worth £30 million.

Jo: When I lived in Hong Kong, I was part of a church group who would spend some of our Saturdays in Shenzhen, just over the mainland Chinese boundary, volunteering in an orphanage for disabled children. Now this was in the days of China's "One Child Policy" and there was little around in terms of a social safety net, so if that one child came along as disabled, many parents sadly took the awful decision to abandon the child. The children in the orphanage had often been found by the side of the road or on the doorstep of the police station.

The orphanage was supported by the state to look after them, but conditions were basic and so a group of enthusiastic volunteers coming in every few weeks to entertain the children and give the overworked staff a hand at feeding time was much appreciated by all.

When the group started visiting the orphanage, it was clear that many of the children just spent their time in their beds or in front of the TV. There was little sense that there was any point in investing in these poor children, who - however kindly meant - were only really subjected to pity and practical management to meet their basic needs.

Then one Christmas, the staff decided to organise a show to thank the volunteers for coming along to help out. They had taught the children to sing songs and learn dances. Nothing had ever been attempted before at the orphanage and both we the volunteers and they the staff were amazed at how well some of the kids had been able to learn things. Having never attempted to do something like this before, it was a complete triumph with the staff saying how much they'd all enjoyed the preparations and that they would be doing more of this in the future. They had seen potential in these kids that no-one else ever had.

In fact, I often think of one of the children in particular who really challenged my understanding of seeing the potential in others. This particular little girl was about seven years old and as well as having physical disabilities, could not talk. She spent her time chewing the long, stiff curtains which adorned every room of the orphanage. I figured that the staff thought she was happy doing that, so left her to it. On one visit, I decided to raise this with one of the carers. "Don't you think we should try to stop her chewing the curtains?" I asked. "Oh no! She loves it," they explained. "Yes, but even so," I tried to point out that it probably wasn't good for her.

The carer took me over to the girl and asked her to show me the curtains. She had chewed incredible designs into them, biting their stiff fabric into grooves: swirls, flowers, faces, animals. They were Picasso-esque in their designs! Absolutely stunning! The carer took me to each room showing me the different curtains. I was totally stunned. I have seen some strange things in my life, but I have never seen anything quite so magical as this incredible art that was coming from this small heavily disabled child. I often wonder what happened to her and what might have happened if someone had supported her to really unleash this potential.

So, this is absolutely a lesson that I take into my professional life. As leaders, in order to create real change in others, we need to ask ourselves: what does this person have inside them? And what kindling can I bring to that spark? As a leader and manager, unlocking such potential is incredibly powerful for your organisation.

When working with a team, I always try to work out what strengths and passions a person really has and encourage them to lean into those more. The bigger your team, the easier it is to move resources around, but even with a small group, look at who really enjoys doing a particular task. Ask you team about how they'd like to share work between them and accommodate passions and talents as much as you can.

One of the many things I love about the Civil Service, is that we are encouraged to contribute to our organisation beyond the core objectives of our day job. This might be volunteering with a staff network, for example a well-being group that works to make the office a better place to work or a charity committee to support good local causes. One such volunteer I have learnt a huge amount from in recent years is a brilliant and passionate lady called Martina Blackman Andersen.

She is employed in our Brussels Embassy supporting UK food and drink companies to export to Belgium. Whilst she's great at her day job, in her spare time, she has transformed our department's approach to racial equality. With a passion for social justice, she has led our staff race network to develop a wide-ranging programme of work, improving our organisation's inclusivity, not just internally for our staff, but championing a programme of promoting businesses who are led by people from groups that traditionally don't benefit as much from such government support. If she had been told to stick to the day job, our organisation and the impact of our work would be so much poorer for it.

Is there someone in your organisation who might have such magic within them that you could set free? Have a look for some of that untapped potential.

Paul: Some of the best experiences in my life have been through seeing the potential in others - but also them seeing it in me. And realising that potential has changed not just my life, but the lives of many others around me.

One organisation I benefited from in my youth is now named Raleigh International. There are some amazing youth organisations in the world based on sports, religion, preforming arts or the armed services for example. These may or may not include elements of pure 'youth work ' (some are more instructional than facilitative, or perhaps more aimed at enjoyment than development), but they all help to build relationships. Raleigh is that sort of organisation and it changed my life, creating a massive ripple effect.

I remember seeing a poster advertising Raleigh, when I was 20 years old. It explained how young people could apply to go on an expedition to a far-off land. An adventure? Count me in!

I ended up on a small Island off the coast of New Zealand named Breaksea Island, killing hordes of rats. Maybe not the adventure I'd expected! But it was to open a new chapter of my life. Our expedition was to save the last remaining Kakapo Birds. The Kakapo is a flightless parrot and at the time there was only 66 of them left in total. (Spoiler alert - there are now over 200!)

Our role was to kill the many (many) non-indigenous rats on Breaksea Island, so that the Kakapo bird could continue to nest there. There were about a dozen of us on the island with this grim task. One of these was a guy named Simon Weston, a young Welshman and Falklands War veteran (who I have mention already).

After a few weeks, with the job done, everyone swam out to a passing fishing boat and were taken to the mainland. Everyone but Simon and I that is. I was ill due to the rats nibbling our food and Simon - incredibly - volunteered to be the one to stay and look after me. A replacement team would be out in a couple of weeks' time, and we could leave then.

Simon used to come over to my tent and by spending quality time with each other - enforced though it was - we discovered a joint passion: we would like to help young people who were struggling when we returned to the UK. Something clicked and we saw that potential in each other and realised that by putting it together, we could make a real difference.

(One day, feeling a bit better, I walked over to Simon's tent. "Simon," I said as I knocked on the tent post. We were on an island at least 20 miles from the next human being. Simon called: "Who is it?")

When we returned to the UK, we started a youth charity named *Weston Spirit* in honour of the determination Simon had shown in overcoming his injuries. The charity went on to be a major part of both our lives and help thousands of young people to overcome adversity and lead successful lives. By seeing and nurturing the potential in each other, we were able to unlock the potential in thousands of others too.

Exploring Potential Exercise

You can use this as a framework for discussing potential with other people. But first of all, try it on yourself. Whether you feel lacking in purpose of not, it's a useful exercise in developing self-awareness. Reflective practice in youth work is not just key to seeing and developing the potential in others, but also in oneself.

1. Ask someone who knows you well to identify three things from the list below that hold you back. Ask them why they chose those three.

- Opportunities
- Self-belief
- Freedom
- Time
- Clarity
- Focus
- Money
- Contacts
- Skills
- Other

2. Do you agree with their reasoning?

3. What are you going to do about it?

4. Note down what action you could take starting today to release more of your potential.

Make judgments, but don't be judgemental

To get the best out of people and unlock their potential, we need to avoid being judgemental. Let us say a bit more about why.

When we judge someone as lacking in some way, we don't open ourselves to learning from them (attribute 1) and can dismiss their potential. We also deny ourselves and others the opportunity of benefitting from their potential strengths. Within modern society, we increasingly see people judging others - especially on social media - which is leading to a breakdown in relationships in families and communities.

By adapting youth work skills of a non-judgemental approach, you will be able to build networks, create new connections and repair broken relationships. You will be able to learn and profit from the potential of those around you in ways you cannot imagine at first glance.

Paul: A few years ago, I was sent a client who was considered to be a tough nut to crack. After our first chat, I noticed that he had scratched his name into my desk while he was waiting for me in my office. My initial reaction was anger. He'd ruined my rather nice desk. But after I'd cooled down, I realised that the desk, my office, myself - everything was in fact there to help him, and people like him. And this was his normal modus operandi: acting out to try to get attention. So instead of getting angry at him, I tried something different. I bought a box of chocolates in a wooded box, scratched his name on the box and sent it to him.

Now this caught him off guard. He was curious. It got him to reflect. Who was this guy who didn't react like everyone else? It led to a conversation, which in due course, led to a breakthrough. Something that others thought couldn't be done. They'd written him off as impossible to deal with.

What I had done was to separate the action from the individual. The phrase "hate the sin, love the sinner" is sometimes used by Christians. In fact, it's not in the Bible, but you get the idea. You can judge that the act is wrong without being judgmental about the individual who carried it out.

I could offer an endless number of stories like this from the world of youth work. For example, a while back we had put together a programme for a group of teenagers from a training scheme in Liverpool. The scheme had warned us off working with two of the lads in the group - Jake and Tosh - who they described as "trouble".

I went in to see the woman who was running the scheme and explained to her how the programme would get the group working as a team and then give them the opportunity to come up with a project to help the community. "It sounds like you'll get them all fired up and bouncing with ideas." Then, in all seriousness, she continued. "It takes us about three weeks to knock that out of them when they come back here." I decided to let the lads on the programme.

There were 12 young people in the group and whilst we felt like we were making progress, it frankly would have been a lot easier without Jake and Tosh. I did wonder if I had made a good judgment call or not. They wandered from being uninterested to being disruptive and back again.

As it was getting near Christmas the group came up with the idea of collecting gifts from local shops and giving them out in care homes. We prepared the young people for the task in hand and got them to think about how they would approach walking into a shop and asking for a gift. We helped the teenagers to think about their language, their confidence and gratitude. Off they went and returned two hours later with boxes of chocolates, jigsaws and ornaments. They were delighted with themselves (including Jake and Tosh) and they couldn't wait to visit the OAPs the next evening.

The next evening arrived, and we piled on the minibus. As we walked into the first home, I was reminding them of appropriate behaviour and language. I walked through the big front doors and up to the reception. I said to the receptionist, "We have come to give some gifts out".

"We?" Queried the receptionist bemused.

I looked around and I was all alone. "One moment please," I said and walked back outside. All the group were standing outside looking terrified. After some persuasion, I got them into the home. I told them we had to be back on the bus in 40 mins, as we had more homes to visit.

The elderly people were lovely, and the young people got a real sense of two-way appreciation. The time flew, the home's staff thanked us, and we were soon back on the bus. The young people were chatting about the people they had met and looking forward to the next stop.

A quick head count before we set off (as always) made me realise we were two heads short. "Who's missing?" I asked. It was Jake and Tosh. My blood ran cold, where are they I thought. What are they up to? Images shot through my mind of them being rude, aggressive, or worse. I ran back into the home. I scanned the main hall and several of the bedrooms, but they were nowhere to be seen.

Finally, looking into a bedroom I saw a sight I would not forget. An elderly man was sitting in a high-backed chair and Jake and Tosh were kneeling on the floor either side of him. The man was crying, and he had tight hold of Jake and Tosh's hands. "Come on, lads." I said quietly.

Jake turned to me and said with tears in his eyes." But his wife died." I realised that I had been being judgmental. Jake and Tosh were great lads who went on to secure good jobs. Last I heard, Jake was working in a care home.

We all have to make judgments, but we all need to be careful that we are not being unjustly judgemental. By taking those lads onto that programme, they made a positive impact on the old folks they visited, it changed their mindset and led to them becoming valuable and valued members of the community.

Jo: We all make quick judgements as shortcuts to get us through the day-to-day efficiently. But we have to be careful in applying quick judgements to people, not just for their benefit, but for our own and for wider society. In fact, being open-minded and not judging others is important for our species to thrive and unfortunately, we are seeing how judgemental and prejudicial attitudes continue to harm our communities.

Society is pulling itself apart with the political left and the right unable to find compromise and middle ground. The gap between the richer and poor is widening. Despite - and because of - immigration into our cities, cultures live apart with limited mixing, causing tensions to build. Communications designed to help bring us together, often create the opposite effect with algorithms pushing polemics, encouraging more extreme views and echo chambers. And thanks to social media, judging others and voicing those judgements online has become the norm, when actually what we need is a coming together and repairing of links.

Jon Yates in his excellent book *Fractured* talks about "People Like Me Syndrome" - that we judge that we are safest with people of equal status and similar backgrounds, but this is toxic for our society as we start to turn against each other. He argues that we need to start "strengthening the glue that bonds our societies, in all their diversity" and that a powerful way of doing this is to be open-minded to people unlike ourselves. This really resonates with me. I couldn't agree more. One of the most inspiring people I've ever met, is a Filipina domestic helper in Hong Kong. A wonderful lady called Liza Avelino. As a senior diplomat working at the British Consulate, many people at first glance found ours a strange friendship, but Liza brought so much to the people around her, to her community, to anyone whose life she touched.

The first time I met Liza, I had signed up for a Sunday hiking group which met to trek up a stream on an outlying island of Hong Kong. I started chatting to Liza while we were waiting for everyone to arrive. She explained that she was one of the hundreds of thousands of Filipina domestic helpers who worked in the city. She looked after the home and children of an ex-pat family. Some of the other hiking ex-pats - the few that had bothered to say hello to Liza - seemed to lose interest at this stage, quickly judging that a "helper" (as they were called in the city) was of little interest to them. But as I continued chatting to her, it gradually became apparent that Liza was someone incredibly special.

She loved to be out in nature, so using her single day off each week, she had taken up hiking. In fact, the day I met her, she was leading our hiking group up the streams and gorges of Lantau Island. Inspired by the mountains, she had started to train for some serious challenges and over the next few years, she hiked up Kilimanjaro, climbed Korea's highest mountain, summited Himalayan peaks...the list goes on. Each time raising thousands of pounds for charities supporting migrant workers and other good causes like rebuilding villages destroyed by the Kathmandu earthquake. Unlike too many of us (who have much great means at our disposal), Liza would save her domestic worker wages to pay for her flight, trek fees and equipment herself. Focusing all her fundraising efforts on others.

Liza had an incredible back story which I was only to learn about years later when I attended the premier of a film made about the lives of migrant workers in Hong Kong called *The Helper*. Liza's was one of the featured stories and as I sat by her in the auditorium, the on-screen Liza explained that she had come to Hong Kong fleeing an abusive husband who probably would have beaten her to death had she stayed much longer. But to leave the Philippines, she had to walk away from her baby twin boys. Now 20 years later, she did not know what had become of them. As we both sat weeping in the movie theatre, she said that she was so sorry not to have told me her story before. She was worried that people would judge her for abandoning her children. I only just had enough words to bat away the unnecessary apology. It just drummed home to me once again how incredible this lady was.

The helper community in Hong Kong - largely made up of migrant workers from the Philippines, Sri Lanka and Indonesia - was treated with wary acceptance. The were needed to keep the city running, but had limited rights. Liza would explain, "Migrant workers, just like everyone else, have a dream. Unfortunately, they are not encouraged to dream." But Liza didn't let that stop her.

She didn't let these challenges hold her back. She delivered (despite being terrified) a TEDx talk on her experiences overcoming adversity and then went on to be a regular motivational speaker. As an inspirational speaker, Liza's experiences made compelling listening. Whatever challenges I was facing in my day-to-day life, they were nothing compared to what she had faced and so she spoke with clarity and credibility. "Don't let your fear, decide your future" is one of my favourites.

She threw herself into a Filipina dragon boat team, then a migrant cricket team, using these opportunities to inspire others in her community to follow their dreams. "Empowered women, empower other women," she would say with a shrug.

We now live in a society struggling with the challenges of migration, with some people still ill-at-ease with migrant workers. We often are judgemental about their worth and potential. But, to quote some of Liza's words: "Migration is a courageous expression of an individual's will to overcome adversity, to live a better life and hope for a brighter future."

I took many lessons from my time with Liza. Too many people just walk by Liza community's without a second glance. But what could we achieve if we paused on making a quick judgement and supported each other to follow our dreams? Almost 10 years on from that first meeting, Liza's story still inspires me to be more resilient, to never give up. But also, to look beyond common prejudices to see the real person. Not to look past someone because they are "just" the cleaner. Those hikers who judged Liza as irrelevant to them that day really missed out.

This approach can also be helpful for professional success in many workplaces. Don't we all want to work for managers who are empathetic, who see the best in people and accept other points of view? As managers, imagine how you could make a difference by taking a non-judgemental approach to your team. How might this play out?

When I arrived in Paris to begin my posting at the British Embassy as head of the international trade team a new contact asked my why most of my team were not diplomats. Out of 35 people in my team, only two of us are diplomats. The rest are people hired locally in France. Most of them French. How can local French people represent the UK? You might ask. Some people assume that only diplomats staff our embassies. In fact, it is the local staff that year after year, decade after decade drive forwards the work of the embassy. The diplomats come in and out, but those people stay, build enduring networks, build the organisational memory. These local hires tend to be more junior grades than the diplomats, but in reality these are the people that really know the place, know the job, know the people, know the challenges and how things work. I've learnt that taking time to really get to know the local team and drawing on their expertise is crucial, not assuming that because I'm more senior and happen to have a flashy passport, I know more than them. I just know and bring different things to the team, but these local staff are the real backbone of our diplomatic missions overseas.

Are there people around you, in your work or in your community that you may have judged too quickly? That might deserve a second glance?

One powerful thing that I encourage all managers and leaders to try is reverse mentoring. This is where - instead of a senior colleague offering advice to a more junior one - the more senior party seeks to learn from the perspective of a more junior member of the team. This helps leaders really test the impact of their approach on different part of the business and helps them understand the organisation much better. One of my reverse mentors is the aforementioned Martina Blackman Andersen, who I credit with a large part of my development in trying to understand racial equality issues in society. What might you be able to learn from someone technically more junior in your company's hierarchy? Give it a try. You might discover a world you never knew existed.

Judgements Exercise: To judge or not to judge, that is the question...(20 minutes)

We all need to exercise good judgement. But we also need to avoid being too judgemental, as it closes us off to seeing the potential in others. Here is an exercise to explore how to avoid being too judgemental. Do it with a partner if you can, to explore different perspectives.

Step 1: Where is your opinion on each of the sets of statements on the spectrum below. The statements are designed as sets of opposites.

1 = totally agree with the statement to the left. 10 = totally agree with the statement to the right.

Beliefs		
All people are of equal value	1 2 3 4 5 6 7 8 9 10	Some people are inferior
You can't trust politicians	1 2 3 4 5 6 7 8 9 10	You can trust politicians
God does not exist	1 2 3 4 5 6 7 8 9 10	We should be devoted to God
Values		
You must be 100% honest	1 2 3 4 5 6 7 8 9 10	It is ok to be somewhat dishonest sometimes
You must be always 100% open with your spouse	1 2 3 4 5 6 7 8 9 10	It is ok to have some secrets from your spouse
You should go above and beyond for your employer	1 2 3 4 5 6 7 8 9 10	Don't do more than you are paid for
Self first	1 2 3 4 5 6 7 8 9 10	Self last
Actions		
I would borrow money without checking with my spouse	1 2 3 4 5 6 7 8 9 10	I would never borrow money without checking with my spouse

I will always back my family	1 2 3 4 5 6 7 8 9 10	I will back people against my family
I am hard working	1 2 3 4 5 6 7 8 9 10	I am lazy
I would be physically aggressive	1 2 3 4 5 6 7 8 9 10	I would never be physically aggressive

Step 2: Note your thoughts against each question:

- How did you come to your above decisions?

- Have your opinions changed over the years?

- Are your views contextual?

- Are people wrong if their beliefs, values and actions are different to yours?

- Do you think you are open minded?

- What is the best way to treat people with beliefs, values and actions different to yours?

- If you completed this with a partner, did you feel uncomfortable discussing your views with them? Why was that?

By avoiding being judgemental and keeping an open mind, we keep ourselves open to the potential in ourselves and those around us.

Conclusion

By exploring your own potential, you can increase your sense of purpose and your positive impact on the world. As a people, we have never felt so lost. This is the way we find our purpose again - delving into ourselves to identify and nurture our own potential, unblocking ourselves and breaking down the barriers holding us back. Then supporting other people to do this. Bringing out the potential in others can change lives and communities. The gift of giving that to yourself and to others is not only deeply satisfying. It will change the world.

In order to get the best out of others though, it sometimes takes a fundamental dimension of youth work: avoiding being judgmental. Avoiding simple judgements of others allows us to remain open to more possibilities, giving us more chance to see the potential that reside in others around us. Open-mindedness creates connections and opportunities.

This is not just about tolerance of difference, but real appreciation of the strengths that other perspectives can bring. We can benefit from this as individuals, but also as communities. Our teams, our societies are stronger when we appreciate their diversity.

Sometimes people fear opinions and ideas different to their own, as it makes them feel uncomfortable. Our brains seek predictability and certainty. But we are about to come to the single most important attribute of a youth worker, which enables them to face whatever comes their way from a firm foundation: integrity.

Attribute 10: Integrity

"If you have integrity, nothing else matters. If you don't have integrity, nothing else matters." Alan K. Simpson

The word "integrity" evolved from the Latin adjective "integer", meaning whole or complete. When used to describe a person, it refers to living by one's values.

When we look around us today, many people feel that some of our leaders are lacking the integrity of previous generations. Maybe we are remembering through rose-tinted glasses, but for centuries, our countries have relied on the leadership of our political, religious and community leaders. But our confidence in them has been eroded in recent decades as political scandals have become more commonplace and science has torn apart faith in the church. The past is gone, for better or for worse.

Populism is on the rise with some politicians increasingly playing to the crowd, rather than truly leading, guided by their beliefs and values.

But integrity is crucial for healthy individuals and healthy societies. It's about taking moral responsibility for your actions. Doing the right thing and following through on commitments. It helps you maintain your dignity and self-respect. It helps ensure societies that are just and fair. If we are to overcome the challenges we face as compassionate human beings, we need to hang on to integrity as a guiding concept. So, to whom can we look to learn about integrity?

Well…the single most important attribute of a youth worker is integrity.

The role of the youth worker is to support young people to live an effective life. Being effective requires this alignment of beliefs, values, and actions. The youth worker is therefore not only required to have integrity themselves, but to foster it within the young people they work with. For example, by looking for any contradictions or hypocrisy that may lead to problems.

To do this well, youth workers must be continually checking and improving their own lives. Not just their working life but their whole life.

Mahatma Gandhi held weekly receptions where people could ask for his for his wisdom and advice. At one such reception, a mother asked how she could get her son to stop eating sweets and eat healthier? Gandhi thought for a moment and then asked the mother to bring the child to a reception in three weeks' time. The mother did this and Gandhi advised the child not to eat too many sweets and to listen to his mother. The mother thanked Gandhi but asked why she had to wait three weeks. Gandhi replied that up until three weeks ago he had been eating too many sweets.

Paul: Youth workers don't have to be angels, we are all a work in progress, but they must be willing to examine and review their beliefs, values, and actions in order to live a purposeful life. I am not saying you can't eat cake, drink and party like it's 1999 (again), but to have integrity you must make sure you are happy with your behaviour or adapt it. This allows you to hold a mirror up to other people's behaviour.

It isn't easy.

Take the example from when I was working for a charity several years ago, our fund-raising lead came to me to tell me that we had been offered £50 in sponsorship from a cigarette company. I discussed with my senior team, and we all agreed we didn't want the money, as it sent the wrong message to the young people with whom we were working. We all went away patting ourselves on the back, congratulating ourselves for "being right". Until our fund-raiser clarified it was actually £50,000. We stopped patting ourselves on the back and reconsidered the benefits we could deliver for that amount of money. We took the money. Would we do the same now? I don't know. We are all on a journey and are learning and growing all the time.

Integrity doesn't mean being fixed, inflexible or dogmatic. It means being self-aware and making a clear choice and sometimes swapping a course of action for something of a higher value.

Integrity also means owning mistakes and apologising when you know you have made a mistake.

A few weeks back, I took a trip in my car to the supermarket. When I arrived there was a line of six parking spaces, the first five of which were designated 'parent and child' by markings on the floor. The end space had no markings and was therefore open to anyone. I parked there and went in to grab some shopping. On my return to my car, I was placing my shopping in the boot when I felt a knock on my shoulder. I turn around to see a middle-aged woman who was professionally dressed in a smart blue top and green trousers.

"I've been waiting for you," she said angrily. "I saw you park there, and you don't have any children." I was quite shocked and wondered if I had made a mistake. I double checked.

"This isn't a parent and child space," I objected.

"Yes, it is." She snarled pointing to the markings of the parking space next to mine.

"No, it isn't." I said pointing under my car.

She looked under my car and was dumbstruck. She had waited 20 minutes and now had nowhere to go with this accusation.

"Are you going to apologise?" I queried.

"No, I'm not," she said, turned and walked off in a huff.

I like to see what I can learn from every unexpected event in my life. How could I have been more effective in that situation? I thought as I drove home. I can't think of anything I would do differently. So, I thought about the woman's behaviour to see if there was anything I could learn from that. There were four things. Firstly, self-righteousness isn't a good look, her manner had an air of superiority. Secondly, instead of making an accusation, ask a question. She could have said: "Excuse me, but have you parked parent and child space?" (This learning point has really helped me in many work and family situations.) Thirdly, if you know you are wrong, apologise and own the mistake. That way you can put the matter to bed. Finally, the saying 'blue and green should never be seen without a colour in-between' is so true. (A bit too catty? Maybe. I don't pretend to be perfect!)

We all make mistakes; we all have discrepancies in our behaviour, and we are all hypocritical at times. To act with integrity is to notice these slips and foibles and improve a little each day.

Jo: Integrity is the first of four aspects of the Civil Service code of ethics (honesty, objectivity, impartiality being the other three). It is defined in the code as "putting the obligations of public service above your own personal interests" which is something that guides many of us in public service. But of course, integrity is a concept much wider than this.

Authenticity

For me, a key part of my integrity as a leader, is being an authentic leader. My style of leadership is one based on genuineness and honesty. I focus on building positive relationships with my team and try to inspire their trust. But what are the key aspects of authentic leadership?

1. Know thyself

To be an authentic leader, you need to firstly know yourself well. This has taken me some time! And is an ongoing process. I have been subjected to many different personality profiling tools during my career. I've lost count of how many times I've done the Meyers Briggs tests (and it has shifted over time). I don't think it matters too much which tools you use, the importance is the discussion and self-reflection that they stimulate. 360-degree feedback is also very helpful. As civil servants, we get this at least once a year. Encouraging people to feed back (anonymously is helpful to allow frankness) with constructive criticism is a great way to understand how you come across to others and the impact you are having on those around you. As well as helping you understand yourself better, you have to commit to considering the feedback and acting on it.

2. Be honest and transparent

This is not about constantly wearing your heart on your sleeve, as we discussed in an earlier chapter on resilience. You should always bring the professional version of yourself to work and if you tend towards extroversion with your emotions, you might need to tone that down in the workplace. All leaders at times will have privileged information about the organisation or individuals (e.g. as part of HR processes) which it might not be appropriate to share with everyone. But where you can be transparent, it is important to be. Studies on Generation Z in particular show they expect their leaders to be honest and authentic with them, not just feed them a corporate line. Without honesty and transparency, you cannot be authentic, and you will lose credibility with your colleagues.

3. Do the right thing

As an authentic leader it is important to be fair. As a civil servant, there's also an obligation to the taxpayer to do the right thing by them. But how do you know what the right thing is? Well, if you have a strongly developed sense of your own beliefs and values, this can take you a long way. I'm not saying that I never have moral dilemmas. Sometimes the way forward isn't as clear as that, but ultimately you will know if your decisions and actions align to your values and beliefs by whether you feel comfortable or not with what you have done. Integrity allows you to sleep well at night.

The Q10 Integrity Checker

We all have things that are private and things which are personal, but do you have any secrets? Things which you don't want people to know because you are embarrassed? Things which you have done or said that you would rather not think about or have brought out for inspection? Why is this? Are there events which diminish your opinion of yourself? Or are you scared that you may be diminished in the opinion of others?

You can hide from others but can't hide from yourself. You may bury something, but it is still there. The best way to deal with these things and keep your integrity is to own the decision, claim the learning and move on. So, if you've got something bothering you about a secret you have or something you've done which doesn't sit right with you, let's look at how you can work on this. This type of honest look at one's issues takes bravery. It might be something you prefer to come back to after further consideration.

Write or think about something you have done, and you would rather not write or think about.

Part A (Your decision)

1.   Do you own the decision you made?
This means to accept that you made that decision, regardless of any mitigating circumstances.

2.   Looking back, do you agree with the decision you made at the time?
Can you understand why you made that decision at that time?

3.   Faced with the same choice today would you make the same decision?

Given what you know now, would you make the same decision in the same situation?

4.   Do you need to make amends with anyone?

If you believe you may have wronged anyone, will you make it up to them?

Part B (Your secret)

5.   Are you keeping your past actions hidden?

Are you clear about your choice to be transparent or not (and with whom)?

6.   Are you ashamed of what you did?

Can you make a distinction between yourself of the past and yourself of the present?

7.   How will you behave if what you did becomes known?

Will you deny, explain, accept, apologise, downplay or other?

Part C (Your development)

8.   What have you learned?

Have you learned anything?

9.   Do you need to change your current behaviour?

Are you likely to repeat your mistakes?

10.   Do you need to make a commitment?

Would you like to put any commitment in place to yourself or others?

Burying your past is not congruous with having integrity. Putting your past right does not require you renouncing all your history, but it does require you coming to terms with what you did yourself and is an opportunity to capture and use the learning.

Parenting with Integrity

Integrity in the parenting realm is particularly relevant. As parents we need to be consistent, true to our word in order to provide structure and instil discipline in the lives of our children. This must come from a place of integrity, or children and young people will not respond positively.

We have already touched a little on this when we considered kindness with strength: young people are crying out for discipline. Not punishment. Let's be clear. Punishment and discipline are two very different things. Punishment is about correction and retribution. It is one way but not the best way of bringing about discipline. Discipline is about standards, focus and commitment. Young people (in fact all people) appreciate knowing where they stand. Discipline enables consistency. If you are not demonstrating discipline yourself and you are not enforcing discipline, being consistent, people - including your children - will lose respect for you.

Paul: The statement "Do as I say not as I do" lacks discipline, lacks integrity and does not work. By keeping to what you say young people know they can believe you. I remember my daughter Siobhan saying to me that she knew she could stop worrying if I said, "Don't worry about that, I will sort it." Whether it was a big thing or a small thing, if I said I would sort it, I would sort it. That was a nice compliment.

My kids Lee and Siobhan usually get along great, but I remember an occasion when they were both mid-teens and they were quarrelling and being nasty to each other. I had to step in and get them to apologise to each other.

"You say it first," grumbled Lee.

Siobhan said, "Sorry, Lee" without much fuss, but Lee dug his heals in and said he hadn't done anything for which he needed to apologise. Having said they should both apologise and given that Siobhan had said sorry, I thought it was important for Lee to apologise too.

"I don't have to say sorry, if I don't mean it." Lee said stubbornly.

"Well, you do now, because you agreed to say it back when you said 'you first' to Siobhan."

There was silence.

"Ok," I decided." If you don't say sorry right now, I am going to pick you up from school tomorrow, wearing your nana's wedding hat."

"I'm sorry, Siobhan!" Lee said quickly, wide-eyed. I don't recommend the overuse of such brinkmanship, but my kids know I'm true to my word. Lee knew that I 100% would follow through!

Conclusion

We have concluded this book with the attribute of integrity, as we feel it is so crucial to an individual's success and happiness, as well as important for the health of communities and societies. Whilst someone with less integrity might seem successful in the short term (e.g. being dishonest for personal gain) this lack of principals or moral code will undermine their relationships and often their peace of mind. For true success and indeed personal contentment, acting with integrity will see you right.

Integrity is often described as "doing the right thing when no-one is watching", but we don't entirely agree, as it's important to do it when others are watching too! It's an opportunity to be a positive role model. And we are all crying out for those.

Conclusion – becoming successful

Youth workers deliver personal and social development, which helps people to be successful through developing their character. The aim of this book is to take you on a personal and social development journey in order to help you to become more successful.

But what does it mean to be more successful? What is the target? This is something that you will want to consider for yourself, but we'll offer you some food for thought before we bid you farewell.

Given that the world is changing so rapidly, it would certainly be very useful to know what we should be aiming for. Our brains crave certainty, but we don't get too much of that in the modern world. If your head isn't spinning, you haven't been paying attention. Some people adopt a deliberate strategy of not paying attention. Not watching the news and not discussing politics, religion or the use of power. Preferring to stay focused on their immediate family, friends, their pet, their garden, their holiday. Trying to escape the uncertainty. It doesn't work. Everything is connected to everything else, so in order to deal successfully with the changes in the world around us - economics, technology, climate and culture – you need a clear target. Something to aim for. A way of making sense of your life. A budding world leader or a hermit must face the same question: what will make my life successful?

Strange as it may seem, many people find life too complex, too busy to pause and ask this question. Preferring to live one day at a time and hope that a lottery ticket will rescue them from the vortex. This can lead to mid-life crises or worse. But it's not surprising that people struggle to define success, define what they are aiming for in life.

Paul: I once asked a group of a dozen 16-year-old girls about their ambitions and five of them said they wanted to be a WAG - the wife or girlfriend of a famous man (usually a footballer). There was nothing about contribution to society, nothing about achievement, nothing about having a positive impact on the world. I am not having a go at the girls. I am just questioning a society that has prepared young people for a world in which they see their success as being a trophy. I am also not having a go at WAGs here as I have never met one. I am sure the reality is a million miles away from what is presented in the media, but it is the notion of a WAG that these teenagers and millions of others aspire to achieve: an easy life where someone else provides the means for their material needs and enjoyment.

And why wouldn't they? We are continually sold a paradigm which states what success looks like. The brands, the looks, the status, the physical prowess, the influencers, the reality TV. Why wouldn't the next generation want to be rich and famous? At least that gives them a clear target.

"I think everybody should get rich and famous and do everything they ever dreamed of so they can see that it's not the answer." Jim Carrey

Rich?

According to Forbes magazine there are now over 2500 billionaires on the planet with a collective wealth of over 12 trillion USD. If money equals success and success equals happiness these people must be living in permanent bliss.

Between us, we have met quite a few billionaires and haven't yet met any blissful ones. Whilst we all need money to live, and money can afford us certain freedoms and powers it doesn't seem to bring happiness. Having little or no money is a struggle, but having too much money will not eliminate worries, it will just generate different ones.

Paul: I once spoke with a man whose role it was to offer support, advice and guidance to people who won the lottery. He said to me, "If they were miserable before they were rich, they will be miserable millionaires." I conclude that money does not equal success any more than a hammer equals a masterpiece or a murder.

Famous?

Paul: In the late 1990s, I took part in a reality TV game show named *Wanted*. My fellow contestant Lucy Renwick and I had to escape capture for several weeks to raise money for charity. After the programme we returned to Liverpool and having been on TV for several weeks people recognised us. I am not saying we were A-list celebrities but for two or three weeks it was very odd to be approached in the supermarket by total strangers who felt they knew me when I had no idea who they were. It gave me the slightest glimpse as to what it is like to be famous. I found it unnerving. Most of us live in a world in which being a stranger is a two-way experience.

So why do so many people want to be famous? Well fame can bring opportunities; it can bring status and it can be a form of power. Some people manage all this quite well. But those who seek fame to give their lives meaning, to find self-esteem or to fulfil a need to be loved will be disappointed. When fame comes as a byproduct of developing a talent, it can be useful but when it is an aim within itself it is the opposite to personal and social development. A very dangerous, very fickle, narcotic.

This doesn't just apply to fame. It is also true when we harbour a desire to be admired and put on a pedestal. Pedestals are remarkably unstable. Being well known, admired or even adored is not a bad thing necessarily but desiring it as an end in itself is vacuous and will be ultimately unsatisfying.

So what is success?

"Success" is a concept we have wrestled with throughout our lives and intensively as we have worked on this book over the last year. This is something you will have to explore for yourself, but we are in the business of giving you food for thought, so here is our answer.

We have come to the conclusion that success is feeling satisfied with your life and that true satisfaction only comes from aligning your beliefs, values and actions – something that you may have noticed as a theme running through this book. If you are doing things not aligned with your beliefs and values, you will feel unfulfilled. We are both fortunate to have careers that align strongly with our beliefs and values. We work on issues that we feel passionate about and prioritise things and people that are important to us. It means that when we consider our lives, we feel satisfied and content with our choices. That's not to say that every day is easy and that we don't worry about things. Of course we do. Such is life. But when asked what we would do if we could do anything in life, we would choose what we do now.

So, our advice is to use the exercises in this book to really work on yourself to ensure you are aligning your beliefs, values and actions.

TAKE ACTION!

You need to align your beliefs and your values with your actions. But let us be clear: the action part is crucial to success.

If you believe that humans are destroying the planet and you believe we can each make a difference you may well value recycling, reusing and energy saving but that does not mean a thing unless you actually take action. It is only at the point of action when you are being effective. You may believe that eating healthily can give you a better chance at a longer and more fulfilling life so you may value not eating fast food and the idea of limiting your sugar intake. But it is only your actions that will make a difference.

Take a family in which everyone loves grandad equally but who actually steps up when grandad needs some care? There is a difference between loving someone and caring for them. The difference lies in action.

And so, your final set of questions.

1.   **What do I need to do or stop doing to improve my life?**

2.   **What is my plan to ensure this happens?**

3.   **Who can help me with this?**

And finally...

Youth workers scrutinise the behaviour of young people and through a non-judgmental relationship, they ask insightful, sometimes uncomfortable questions so that young people can learn to refine their own thoughts, feelings, beliefs, values and actions for the rest of their lives.

If you never had a kind and wise youth worker when you were young, don't worry. Work on developing the attributes highlighted in this book, and you will be applying the lesson from youth work to your own life and to the lives of those around you. In this way you will have a more enjoyable and purposeful life, taking your place amongst the best of us.

Acknowledgements

Paul and Jo would like to acknowledge the following people who were not mentioned in the text but each in their own way has supported the creation of the book.

Our families and friends for their love

Mervyn Kaye for his encouragement and reflections

Patrick Turner for his editing and suggestions

Charlotte Brookes for cover and chart wizardry

Robin Sieger, Tom Fletcher and Jon Yates for their publishing advice

Chris Barton for his support and insights

Steph Harrison (Chair of Vibe) for being a role model

Mick Riley and the boys from the parachute regiment for the laughs

Steph Howard (Paul's 10-year spin instructor) for being inspirational

Tim Loughton for his belief in people

Kylie Noonan for her friendship

Windsor Leadership for endless inspiration

Gavin, Yannick and Idil for their early feedback

All the staff and young people at Vibe UK for providing hope

For our many brilliant colleagues alongside whom we are honoured to work

Author Biographies

Paul Oginsky has been dedicated to the development of societal well-being for over 30 years.

Throughout his career he has designed many character education programmes for young people including *On Your Marks* for the Dame Kelly Holmes Trust, *Reach for the Sky* for Sky TV, *Weston Spirit* with Simon Weston MBE and *Think Big* for O2. He has worked as a government adviser on youth policy and led on the development of the National Citizen Service programme. He is also the Founder of PDP UK, a training organisation delivering programmes to support people with their mental wellbeing. He is CEO of Vibe UK, which supports young people across Merseyside to achieve better outcomes by building positive relationships with themselves and others.

Paul once won £20,000 on a TV game show, has run 10 marathons, parachuted 84 times, is a qualified electrician, a black belt in karate and many years ago, took part in an expedition to save the kakapo bird. He is a regular media commentator on issues impacting young people.

Jo Hawley is a senior civil servant who has worked for the Department for Business and Trade, Foreign Commonwealth & Development Office, Department for Education and Cabinet Office. She has represented the UK overseas on diplomatic postings to Brussels, Hong Kong, Guangzhou and Paris and has picked up more than a handful of foreign languages on her travels.

She worked with Paul on National Citizen Service, moving the scheme from pilot to national rollout and developing a deep appreciation of youth workers in the process. She is an experienced coach and mentor, with a focus on under-represented groups in the Civil Service.

Jo is a working mum who has done more parachute jumps than Paul, is catching him up on marathons, but has no idea what a kakapo bird is. She spends too much of her time on Instagram writing her royal history blog and is a museums addict.

About Vibe UK

The youth charity I lead is named Vibe UK and if you can offer it a little support, we will help young people to build their self-esteem, build better relationships and be proactive in their communities. I really believe in this charity because I can't solve all the problems of the world, but by helping young people to align their beliefs, values and actions, maybe they can. They will become more effective, and then they will become our best hope for the future. A donation to Vibe UK is an investment in a better world.

To find out more please visit **www.vibe.org**

Thank you
Paul

Printed in Great Britain
by Amazon

54882787R00126